Out
of
Step

First they came for the Communists,
    But I was not a Communist so I did not speak out.

Then they came for the Socialists and the Trade Unionists,
    But I was neither, so I did not speak out.

Then they came for the Jews,
    But I was not a Jew, so I did not speak out.

And when they came for me,
    There was no one left to speak out for me.

——Martin Niemöller

OUT OF STEP

*my young life as a resister
in Nazi Germany*

by Gisela Dewees

DeForest Press
Elk River, Minnesota

Permission gratefully acknowledge for the following:
    Back cover quote of Adolf Hitler taken from *Voice of Destruction* by Hermann Rauschning. Used by permission of Pelican Publishing Company, Inc.
    The maps on pages 12 and 160 from the U.S. Holocaust Memorial Museum's on-line Learning Center (www.ushmm.org/learningcenter), courtesy of the U.S. Holocaust Memorial Museum, Washington, DC.
    Quote from Martin Niemoller on page 2 as it appeared in Franklin Littell's forward to *Exile in the Fatherland, Martin Niemoller's Letters from Moabit Prison*, edited by Hubert G. Locke (Grand Rapids, Michigan: William B. Eerdman's Publishing Company, 1986).
    Excerpts from "Dietrich Bonhoeffer" used in sidebars on pages 126 and 222 written by Victoria Barnett.

Published by:
DeForest Press
P.O. Box 154
Elk River, MN 55330 USA
www.DeForestPress.com
Toll-free: 877-441-9733
Richard DeForest Erickson, Publisher
Shane Groth, Editor in Chief

Cover design by Linda Walters, Optima Graphics, Appleton, WI

ISBN 1-930374-12-7
Printed in the United States of America
09 08 07 06 05   5 4 3 2 1

Library of Congress Cataloging-in-Publication Data

Dewees, Gisela, 1925-
  My young life as a resister in Nazi Germany / by Gisela Dewees.
    p. cm.
  ISBN 1-930374-12-7
  1. Dewees, Gisela, 1925- 2. Young women—Germany—Biography. 3. Anti-Nazi movement—Germany—Biography. 4. Germany—History—1918-1933—Biography. 5. World War, 1939-1945—Personal narratives, German. 6. Germany—History—1933-1945. I. Title.
  DD256.3.D495 2005
  943.086'092—dc22

2004022226

Dedicated with love to my children
Michael
Barbara Christina
And John Garrett.

And to Odi's children
Anna Regula
and Christiane.

And to Hans's children, never conceived.

About the Author

 Gisela Dewees attended public schools in Berlin, Germany, in the 1930s. She was denied permission to finish and take her college prep finals because of her refusal to join the Nazi youth group *Bund Deutscher Mädchen*. During WWII she trained as a nurse in the cities of Berlin and Schwäbisch Gmund.

She has continued to fight for those who have no voice since coming to the United States in 1947. She was appointed by the governor as a member of the New York State Commission for Human Rights and served as a board member of World Affairs Council, a group that worked with world hunger and the United Nations. She co-founded the Committee of Concern, Broome County, to educate and promote concern in areas of peace, civil liberties, and the cessation of the nuclear arms race. She was also cofounder and publicity chairman of the William C. Moore Chapter of CORE (Congress of Racial Equality). Bill Moore, her friend, was murdered in Gadsen, Alabama, the first white victim of the Civil Rights Movement.

Contents

Preface

We old people prefer to reminisce rather than look ahead. Perhaps by sharing I can help to keep a horror-filled history from repeating itself. I would also like to encourage others not to be embarrassed or afraid when they know they should march out of step, even if they stumble and fall.

Publisher's Preface

Imagine you are a German citizen in Berlin in 1940. The altar in your church is covered not with the usual paraments, the cross, the Bible, or the presence of the German flag, but with a sword, a standing copy of Adolf Hitler's *Mein Kampf,* and the swastika. Your pastor is no longer allowed to preach, for the intention of the State is to have pulpits used for orations given by agents of the Third Reich. Hitler's ultimate goal was to replace all current religion with the ancient Germanic gods of Odin, Thor, and Freia.

By 1940, Hitler's grip on Germany was secure and he was reaching out to control the world. The genocidal movement on all Jews, the Final Solution, was in full force. Countless numbers of people, young and old, had already been sacrificed on the altar of purity and perfection. Meanwhile, there were small groups of resisters in Germany from a variety of faiths and denominations that struggled to survive and maintain their loyalty to a conscience of justice. The Confessing Church was a small movement of such people.

Gisela Harnisch was a teenage girl in Berlin during those years. Her father was Pastor Wilhelm Harnisch, who, with Niemoeller and Bonhoeffer, was an active member of the Confessing Church in opposition to the Hitler-supported Reich Church. Through Gisela's eyes and exceptional portrayal, we are given this view of a courageous family inside the Germany of World War II.

As the world approaches the 60th year since the end of World War II, it is with deep pride that we share a part in the telling of another life-story by one who, at the time, was keenly aware and perceptive, and who now is still alive and part of us today. This is a phenomenal story, well told by one who, after the War, brought her talents to serve others in America.

It is through the memories and words of people like Gisela that some of us will remember and others of us will learn…so none of us will forget those who have no voice.

Richard DeForest Erickson
DeForest Press, Inc.

Paradise Darkens

1929 to 1931

1

Our young years are our longest years, and mine happened to be rather turbulent.

I was a pigtailed four-year-old named Gisela, and it was 1929. The setting was a small, red brick village in northern Germany. It was nestled into seemingly endless pine forests that had clearings of purple heather, white birches, and an occasional stand of ancient oaks.

My home was a sprawling, light-gray washed farmhouse that had long been converted into the Lutheran parsonage. Dark green

Gisela

wooden shutters shaded the many windows, and a small vine-covered veranda hid the front entrance. Little flower gardens flanked the five, worn stone steps, which led up to the veranda and the massive front door.

The entire house was of stone, with many cool, dark rooms. The guestrooms and the maids' quarters were upstairs, circling the huge attic. The attic smelled so sweet—in summer and fall of drying fruit strung up just under the ceiling, and in winter of freshly boiled and starched laundry that caressed your face if you walked on your toes.

The cellar, too, was dry and immense. Many shelves lined the thick walls. They were loaded with home-canned fruits and vegetables and jams from our gardens, as well as canned meats, which some faithful farm women brought us.

The house was situated just where the highway entered the village, where the road became cobblestone. The front windows faced the dark, comforting forest, while the rear windows, including those of the playroom, faced the backyard. It was the kind of yard one can visualize forever through tears of hopeless longing for one's youth.

The yard was a holdover from former farming days, and my parents' love for animals was reflected in the flocks of fowl roaming it: geese and ducks, chickens and turkeys. A long barn with many stalls and bins of feed corn and hay flanked the yard on

My parents with Odina (Odi), my older sister, in 1923

the left, while the right was walled and lined with cherry, apple, and plum trees planted by Father. Oh how they bent in the late summer with fruit we helped to pick! And what a sea of blossoms in the spring! The little gate at the far end of the yard—where the teeter-totter stood—led into the park-like garden, complete with a brook that separated it from rows of berry bushes and strawberry and vegetable beds.

But best of all was the center of the yard, where a huge lilac bush shaded the fresh-water pump and a dog hut. The pump handle was a great tool to test my strength as I attempted to fill pails of water for the maids. And the hut was home to the beloved "Peter," named after the popular card game "Black Peter." And black he was, and huge—a giant schnauzer, and my friend. I sat next to him by the hour, running my fingers through his curly hair and keeping an eye on my little brother, Hans-Reinhard.

Hans was two years younger than I. Golden curls framed his angelic little face from where large, dark eyes watched you intently. He was my smaller shadow and followed me everywhere. I would always protect him, come what may! Or did I feel so protective only as we got older? But it seems to me now that I always needed his closeness, and that he needed my strength from the very beginning.

And then there was my sister, two years older than I, named Odina, or Odi for short. She was pushing her doll carriage close by me. I hated that doll. It had real hair, its long-lashed lids opening and shutting on its porcelain face as one laid it down and sat it up. It also had dresses of lace. I had only gotten a *Käte-Kruse* baby doll, stuffed and painted, for Christmas, while Odi danced around the tree with her new lady doll.

Hans age 2, Gisela age 4, Odi age 6

Grown-ups always told me not to be envious of my sister's things. They said that some day I would catch up with her and get all nice things, too, with new clothes instead of her hand-me-downs. But it seemed to me that I never, ever caught up with her, and that she was always brighter and more popular, too. Perhaps a second little girl like myself had to have been a disappointment to any family that longed to have a boy. Always my envy mixed nastily into my love for her.

We usually had two maids carrying the brunt of our large household and the many guests and animals and gardens. They also saw to our childish needs. They were simple and warm farmers' daughters, who often held us close when we felt sick or frightened. I felt that they loved me best. Perhaps my sunny, trusting nature made them feel special in return. I learned early that it was much easier and more fun to be with less-educated people than those in my family. They did not expect one to be continuously witty and on one's intellectual toes: they simply accepted one and expected little more than smiles. In that class-conscious society, the "lower class" was always the much more appealing company to me.

I remember that one of the maids took me home with her once to another village. She bought me a lovely dress and taught me how to be the flower girl at her sister's wedding. Then one of the most embarrassing moments of my life occurred: I tripped on the aisle, right in front of the bride, and all the flowers spilled out of my little basket. I remember thinking that surely the whole congregation would hate me forever—but the entourage just stopped a moment, and I was gently picked up and saw only smiling, friendly faces, and no one ever spoke of it to me.

Gisela with
Father's hat & cane

But I must return to the lilac bush. Mother is calling us into the house for dinner, which was always served at noon. She was a stately, beautiful, raven-haired lady. Though her hair was tied in a severe bun at the back of her head, she fashioned ringlets with a hot iron every morning. They covered her forehead above her large, dark eyes. Cheekbones, nose and mouth were chiseled to perfection. She walked so upright, with a whale-boned corset tightly hiding all curves under flowing white summer dresses and severe, black winter suits.

She was a complex human being with an extremely brilliant mind. The oldest of five children, she had to be

My mother as a bride,
about 1915

very responsible at an early age. Her parents were deeply religious, and her father was an incredibly bright man. He received his doctorate in economics at an early age, taught for a few years and then became director of a string of paper factories that he partly founded himself. He located and managed them in Holland, Italy, and even in Russia. His wife, my beloved grandmother, had been the prettiest girl in her hometown, though she never reached intellectual heights. She had a heart of gold, and put up patiently with the numerous moves and many household difficulties in her life. My mother learned and spoke fluently four languages, to which she added Latin later on. She taught math to her little brothers, and she was fully expected to take over her maiden aunts' private *lyzeum* (school) as director and owner some day. She was one of only a handful of female students at various famous German all-male universities, braving the students' hostility and her professors' mistrust.

She earned her doctorate in natural science despite all obstacles, even after two of her three beloved brothers had been killed in World War I. Only as an adult did I realize how hard it must have been for her to give up all dreams of independence and further research, and instead to become a devoted pastor's wife, dedicating her life to him and his work, becoming a shadow to a great man instead of becoming great herself. Mother hid her brilliance, and only availed us of it years later when helping us with our homework.

Yet there was another, darker side to Mother. Somewhere in her family there had to have been a streak of paranoia. She exhibited some of it, but luckily not as much as her younger sister, Annie. Annie had become a professor of mathematics but had suddenly begun to beat up her students. Aunt Annie eventually had to be institutionalized for life. My mother's sudden outbreaks of hostility to us and to Father, her constant accusations and suspicions of thievery, her suspecting Father of unfaithfulness…I shied away from her hectic, unforeseen embraces. I loved her, but I feared her, also. Yet her commitment to Father's struggles, especially against the Nazi regime later, where it took the courage of a lion-hearted human from both of them, she time and again regained my respect and admiration.

Mother met Father while he, too, was working on his doctorate in natural science at the university in Halle. With his usual bravado, he had entered a huge cage full of rats when Mother first saw him. She begged him to get out of the cage before he got bitten, and he laughed and said he would do so if she would promise him a kiss. I doubt if she kissed him—she was so prim and proper and had turned away dozens of students and teachers who were fascinated by her beauty and brains. But so they met. His decency, good humor, wit, and deep faith drew her to him. They became engaged.

Perhaps all of this is not too unusual, but what follows is: They were engaged for a full six years because his parents disapproved of their marriage. Probably because Mother came from a "manufacturing" background rather than a clergy family, as Father's family had been Lutheran clergy way back into history. So Father then added the study of theology to his sciences, and became a clergyman, while Mother taught, did research, or tutored the children of high nobility. They finally married the day after World War I ended, in the absence of his parents.

Father in his study, about 1915

I never knew much about Father's childhood except that it was not a happy one. He finally told Odi much about it as he was about to die. His parents were unbending and stern, almost to the point of cruelty, especially his mother. He had a brother named Siegfried, a sister Odina, nicknamed Oda, and an adopted brother, a Jewish orphan named Alexander. They played no part in my early childhood, so I will get back to them later.

What made Father's entire youth especially hard was a major physical handicap. The midwife at his delivery had dislocated his right hip badly, and an irresponsible surgeon had operated on it with unsterilized instruments. The infection spread and spread, and he suffered 12 more operations before the infections were finally halted. By that time his right leg was so badly shortened that he had a built-up boot to wear. He also had to be privately tutored most of his youth. He limped badly, even with a cane. Father was never, ever without pain, but he never complained to any of us, though we sometimes heard him moan.

He was deeply religious and tried always to practice what he preached. His idols were the Good Samaritan and Martin Luther. His own pain had made him very aware of other peoples' suffering. His parents' dictatorial cruelty made him a persistent champion of the rights of others, as well as of justice and fairness, often to the point of near self-destruction.

Yet, despite his great knowledge and caring, he never really ever knew me. But I digress, and I will now return to the little village of my youth.

The forest was full of deer, boar, and pheasant. Germany's last emperor (by now in exile in Holland) had been a fanatic hunter. He had built a lovely little castle in a clearing close to our house for the sole purpose of

Emperor Wilhelm's hunting castle

entertaining there his various hunting companions before and after the hunts. We children shunned the castle, despite its many little turrets and the great moat, because it was to us a symbol of destruction of wildlife. Since the emperor spent so many weekends there, he decided to build a church nearby for his Sunday visits. To match his ego, he built an immense, gothic structure, which arose like a giant from the flat fields around it. The church was connected to our house and to his castle by a small footpath, while another path led into the village center.

This huge "house of God" was of course much too big for the few village faithful who wanted to hear Father's sermons, and his voice thundered and echoed throughout the immense edifice as he preached.

Here he baptized us three children. And because his parishioners were a very superstitious lot—complete with hex signs on their barns and a village "witch"—Father decided to make sure that each of us children had 13 godfathers and godmothers present at our Baptisms. This, of course, got to be more difficult to accomplish when our parents prepared for Hans's Baptism. But somehow they managed to collar the last of their college-days buddies for the purpose. The number 13, of course, was to prove to the villagers that we babies would not be struck by lightening…

Those early years in the country were the sunniest of my life. I believe I overtrumped even my parents in affection and caring for animals. The yard was teeming with them. The house just had one small pet, an affenpinscher dog, but the barn held a horse, and at times sheep. A kennel held four gorgeous, large black German shepherd dogs, to whom we could throw morsels of food directly from our playroom window. And, of course "Peter," and hundreds of baby fowl in the spring.

The church Emperor Wilhelm built, where Father preached.

The sheep had been a gift of baby lambs for each of us one Easter morning. Odi got a black one, Hans's was brown, and mine was snow-white. Odi paid little attention to hers, but Hans and I spent every available hour with our lambs. We bathed and brushed and fed them, and they frolicked with us on long ropes in the yard. And after we all got tired of playing, we rocked them gently to sleep in their stalls. But one morning I found my little lamb dead in the stall. No one knew what had happened, it just did not wake up. I loaded it into my doll carriage and then sat on the teeter-totter with it in my lap. I petted it and shooed the flies away until a maid came out of the house and gently carried my little lamb away. My family said the lamb was with God now—but I hated God for taking it.

Our horse was yellow and named Fritz. Father had bought it from Gypsies, and we soon realized that this beautiful, citrus-colored animal was probably the meanest horse that had ever pulled a carriage. Since a carriage was the only means of transportation for Father to get to several other villages under his pastoral care, and since we could ill afford to buy another horse, we were stuck with Fritz. With everyone else much too scared to approach the rearing beast, Father's courage was—as always—a shining example to us, as he soothed the monster and rigged him to the carriage. The flailing hooves once sent one of our German shepherds, Ada, flying through the air. It took a skilled vet several months to restore the dog, via much complicated surgery. Interestingly enough, this dog had as much courage as her master: She was barely able to walk again when she tried to bite the leg that had kicked her...

Before he had the horse and carriage, Father rode a bike to the outlying villages. The village smith adjusted the

With Father on front steps

pedals to Father's short leg, and two of the German shepherds were reined to the handlebar to pull Father when his leg got tired. Of his many adventures, as told often by village folk, the one I liked best went as follows:

To perform a wedding in an outlying village, Father had locked the two dogs— still tethered together—in a farmer's barn and had walked the rest of the way to the church. As he was about to pronounce the couple man and wife, his two canines— who had dug themselves out from under the barn door—

had followed his scent to the church. They raced happily through the open church door and headed for Father at the altar. One went left around the bride, the other right around the groom. The couple hit the floor simultaneously, and bedlam broke out with the dogs barking hysterically...

Inventiveness, coupled with total disregard of conventional mores, was one of Father's outstanding qualities. He even painted his pigeons once with non-toxic paint in parrot-like colors to make it more difficult for the farmers to steal them and add them to their own flocks.

To protect Hans and me, I became very brave for such a little girl. There was the gander in the yard when the geese were allowed out to feed on the grass. He guarded his flock with great zealousness, especially during breeding season. He was big and prone to attack humans. The maids were too afraid to go out there to hang up the laundry, and Hans and I dared not to reach the teeter-totter or the swings. One day as I stood by the playroom window and watched the gander strutting, I decided that I should be as brave as Father when he rigged up Fritz. I fashioned myself a switch from a willow branch in front of the house and ventured into the yard. As I determinedly approached the teeter-totter, the white fury raced toward me with outspread wings, hissing viciously. I faced him squarely and swung my switch back and forth in front of me and hissed back at him as hard as I could. He stopped a few feet away from my whistling switch, still hissing and neck stretched out. Then I walked slowly toward him swinging the stick—and he backed up, all the way to his flock. Now I victoriously climbed onto the teeter-totter. The creature never pursued Hans and me again, and the maids followed my example with my little switch. Without my knowledge, Father had stood in the barn door and had watched my gander taming. He had even taken a photograph of the scene.

My courage was at times misplaced, though. I was nearly five in June 1930. The family was invited to a baptismal meal at a farmer's house. After gorging myself on sweet cakes to my heart's content I became bored with all that grown-up talk and the total absence of toys. So I wandered into the farmyard, where a guard dog was tied up. He was eating leftovers from the feast. I had been warned never to approach an eating dog, not even our own. But I got just close enough to him so he could reach me. He did—like lightning he was upon me, and as I turned to flee his jaws closed on the back of my right knee. I screamed and fought but he dragged me toward his hut. The adults raced out of the house to rescue me, but the back of my knee was a bloody mess, besides the tooth marks in front. Luckily, the young village doctor's house was right next door, and he clamped my gaping wounds shut while his beautiful wife stuffed my mouth with chocolates. The dog's teeth had just missed the large tendon or I would have had a stiff leg forever.

I had learned a bitter lesson, as I had to spend a month now on a lounge on the front veranda, with Hans keeping me company. Even Odi felt sorry for me. She went daily to the brook where she caught little minnows and pollywogs to bring to me in canning jars of water.

Just recently I discovered notes my mother had made. They contained some remarks I made when I was four and five, which evidently amused the family. But they speak now to me about me…

"Grandmother, please don't water the flowers so much. You will make them aquaphobic."

"Father is equally as intelligent as I am."

When someone asked, "Gisela, where do you live, next to the church?" "No, next to the big gate to our yard."

"Father hit a bunny with the carriage! Luckily it was not the Easter Bunny, because it was much too small to lay eggs."

"Grandfather, you should not open your mouth. You look much prettier when you are not scolding."

When saying good-bye to my grandfather: "Grandfather, give my best to your grandmother."

When our maid, Sybille, said to me: "Don't always step into the worst mud!" I replied, "I cannot help it if the mud puts itself exactly where my feet are."

"Right, grandmother? When I get to be six years older I will become a man!" (How I had always longed to be a boy!)

"Father, if I had a moustache like yours we could scratch one another nicely."

When Hans interrupted me: "Hans, will you please be quiet! One does not speak when grown-ups speak!"

"Your name cannot be Harnisch, Hans. Harnisch is my name. We cannot both have the same name!"

A maid asks, "Gisela, why are you laughing?" I respond, "About my happiness."

"Odi, you forget everything! You will become a for-get-me-not!"

To the dog: "Pfui, shame on you! The whole stable floor is dirty! You never wipe your feet!"

When a chicken had died: "It shouldn't have. Baby chicks might die because they don't know any better. But big chickens should know better!"

When Odi said to me, "Just you wait 'til you start school. The teacher will spank you because you are so stupid." "Then I will scream his pants full!" I said.

When Odi asked, "Do you like green beans?" I replied, "Don't be so nosy!"

At a godfather's wedding, Gisela says to the groom, "And now you will marry me, yes?"

My parents needed a well-earned rest from us. And because I was to start school in this fall of 1930 already, it was decided it would be good especially for Hans and me to learn to play with other children, rather than only with each other. So the three of us were shipped off to a *Kinderheim*, about two hours by train from us. It was located in a "salt spa" called Elben. A huge white building greeted us, surrounded by meadows and playgrounds.

I am sure that this institute had the best intentions of being beneficial to children of ages three to eight. But being typically German it left much to be desired. We three were immediately separated by age, and I only saw Hans and Odi at mealtime. And even then we had to sit at different tables from each other. To outdoor fun and games we were also marched in different groups and at different times.

The spa had warm salt springs, which were supposed to work wonders on the human body. But on children's bodies full of sores from roughhousing, the salt worked only agony.

And then there was cod liver oil on tablespoons, which nurses shoved into our mouths mornings as we were marched by them. Woe to us if we gagged or spit it out! I remember clearly a little girl's tongue coming off in sheets when a nurse had mistakenly opened a bottle of acid. The girl was just two behind me, and her screams are forever burned into my mind.

I must not forget the sunlight-lamps either, under which we danced to children's tunes wearing nothing at all except dark goggles, until one day another little girl stepped on broken glass hidden in the deep pile of the rug. After that, at least shoes were permitted.

But worst were the nights! We laid on our hard bunk beds in dorms which smelled like hospitals, listening to the sobbing of homesick children all around us, until we sobbed ourselves.

We three felt utterly abandoned by our parents. What few times I managed to talk to Hans were strenuous because I spent every minute trying to convince him that we would be rescued soon.

After what seemed to us an eternity, but was probably only a few weeks, they came to take us home. And in great style! Father had in the meantime sold Fritz (cheaply), and the carriage also. He had purchased a car! And he had learned to drive it, too! We jumped into it overjoyed, barely managing a polite "good-bye" to the nurses and teachers, who were probably relieved to be rid of this depressed trio. And away we went towards home.

But there was one more obstacle to overcome—the wide, deep Elbe River, which had become a raging monster after heavy rains. It was night now and we stopped at the ferry pier. Father got out and rang the big brass bell. But nothing happened, no ferrymaster appeared. We waited and rang and waited. "Enough," said Father, "we must turn around. The ferrymaster is evidently asleep in the village behind us."

But turning around was not that simple. It had begun to rain again in heavy sheets. The banked road behind us had become a mudslide, and Father made us all get out as a precaution. Mother was holding us shivering kids as we watched Father backing up. When he tried to turn around, the wheels lost their tracking on the muddy road, and

Our first car in front of the parsonage

slowly but surely the car slid backwards down the bank toward the broiling Elbe. Mother screamed, "Wilhelm, stop!" And we screamed, "Father, stop! Get out!" But he stayed in the car, and miraculously the wheels stopped exactly at the water's edge! We all said a prayer of thanks and then helped to push the monster back up the bank to safety. We reached the village soaked and shaking and woke up the drunken ferrymaster.

The car made life a lot easier for all of us, and especially for Father, of course. Sometimes he would allow us to accompany him as he proudly drove on the *chaussee* and through the woods to the neighboring villages. There is a picture in my mind that followed me all my life: a starry, summer night as we returned slowly through the forest so as not to disturb the wildlife. And there it was—a large herd of "spotted" deer, which are almost as large as elks, in their bright red coats dotted with pure white. They looked at us curiously and then continued grazing in the clearing by the road—bucks, does, and even half-grown fawns. We whispered and I held Hans tightly while he also looked in awe.

From 1929 until 1931, although home still seemed safe and friendly, there were gathering storm clouds on the horizon. Even we children became more and more aware of the post-war depression as more and more jobless men appeared at our door. At first they fascinated us with their stories of adventures as stowaways on freight cars and as highway tramps. But many did not speak at all, and were terribly embarrassed about their need to beg for help. We searched their gaunt, unshaven faces, their missing teeth, their haunted eyes, and tried to make them feel at home as quickly as possible. Mother washed and bandaged their bleeding feet, the maids washed and mended their clothes, and Father replaced many of their rags with his own clothes. We children served them the hot meals or offered them toys if they had children somewhere at home. Father insisted that they worked for an hour, hacking kindling wood or doing something else. He felt everyone should try to earn their keep, if for no other reason than to regain dignity. There were no jobs to be had in our village. And many village folk were angry at my parents for attracting "trash." One night we finally did get robbed, obviously by someone who had cased us and even knew the dogs well enough to keep them quiet. But none of this deterred us from aiding all desperate strangers.

The village was split into two camps as far as their pastor was concerned. The smaller camp consisted of loyal, warm and moral folk who adored our parents and even us children and who deeply appreciated Father's efforts to aid and educate them and to be friends with them on an equal footing. But the other camp—much larger, of course—consisted of cynical, immoral, and even criminal elements, along with the rich who did not want to share. This parish was a microcosm of our parish later in Berlin, and perhaps of all of Germany in general, and maybe even of the whole world. The decent people will always be a tiny core within the hard-boiled human race. But without this core the world would long have destroyed itself.

I was horrified when I found out that many of the village youth were wildlife poachers who did their bloody thievery with traps and flashlights and guns in our forest. The forester seldom caught them, and the police seldom prosecuted those caught. The only village constable seemed to fear for his own life if he cornered a villain. There was no excuse for this illegal slaughter as they all were part of a planting and meat-raising community.

Another horrifying example of village callousness is also vividly engraved in my mind. One dark fall evening we spotted a brightly-lit airplane in the sky and called Mother so she could see it, too. Then we heard a crack. An hour later the village nurse came and told us that the plane had crashed in the forest, not too far from us. Then she hurried there to see if she could aid the wounded. But all were dead, and she saw several youths running from the grisly scene, loaded with stuff they had stolen from the corpses such as leather jackets and boots... The area newspaper ran the story the next day, but no one was ever caught.

Father had begged the village in vain for years to buy a run-down, deserted farmhouse and turn it into a kindergarten for their often badly neglected and bored children, and to use as a summer haven for city kids. But the village "fathers" steadfastly refused to grant the funds. So in the spring of 1930 he decided to use his own family's last funds, which were to have been our inheritance some day, as I just noted in some family papers. He had the building renovated, and there were now bright playrooms, a kitchen, and living quarters for a kindergarten teacher (employed by the Lutheran Church), along with meeting rooms for the village fathers, and even guest rooms. The big yard was remodeled into lawns, playgrounds with sandboxes, and swings. He called it the Elizabeth Haus. Hans and I had been perfectly happy with each other's company and that of our pets. But we obediently attended kindergarten now and tried valiantly to make friends there with the village children.

One day we heard screams and laughter from the far end of the grounds. We ran to see what the trouble was. The laughter, it turned out, came from five to six boys, and the screams from a younger boy. The gang had grabbed him by his arms and legs and forced his back onto a tall ant heap, crawling with furious red, biting ants.

I lit into the gang without hesitation, while Hans screamed for adults to help. By the time they got there I, too, was getting up from the ant heap.

As far back as I remember, Father had always tried to make very sure that none of our family should make others feel inferior. And he decided one day that Hans should not look different from the village boys. He personally took him to the village barber, where the golden curls were sheared off all the way down to the scalp, for most village kids had short hair because of lice. Odi and I were stunned when he brought a totally uglified, tearful little brother back to us, who hid in dark rooms for days so as not to be seen by anyone. It took a lot of consoling on my part to coax him out. I believe even Mother was shocked, but none of us

Hans after his haircut at the Elizabeth Haus

dared openly to debate "democratic principles" with Father. Ironically enough, the village women were just as horrified when they saw "parson's little angel" so disfigured. The village boys ran after him and yelled, "Baldy! Baldy..."

In the fall of 1930 I started school at the age of five. In order for a child to look forward to the first day of school, the parents presented the child with a "sugar cone." This was a large gilded and lace-covered cardboard cone filled with sweets. And, typical for the German class system, the richer the parents, the bigger the cone, which was taken to school on the first day to be judged and admired by all. Two years earlier my sister had received her cone, which, though not too large, had been ardently admired by me. And now it was my turn! I awoke on my big day to a cone by my bedside that was not even half the size of my sister's. It was surely the smallest cone the village kids had ever seen! To this day I have not figured out why. Perhaps the family had run out of money because of the ever-costing Elizabeth Haus, or Father had once more decided to teach the village a lesson in humbleness (and me, too). But to me it was "proof" once again that they preferred my sister…I pretended to have forgotten to take my cone to school.

The almost two years I spent in that little brick village school were amazingly uneventful. There were only two rooms in it, and mine was for the younger children. It was generally quiet in there and the children fairly well behaved. Not behaving meant getting one's knuckles hit with the teacher's long measuring stick. I don't remember ever getting spanked, and in fact I adored my young and nice-looking teacher with the odd name of Mr. Nagel ("nail"). I soon discovered that math was simply not to my liking, and I never did master a decent handwriting, either. Drawing pictures was also not my strength. But spelling and story writing appealed to me, and singing and sports, also.

My teacher taught us to color all vowels of the alphabet in different colors as we practiced writing them with crayons on our little blackboards (which always had a wet sponge attached to it for quick erasure). This had an interesting effect on me: for the rest of my life I pictured all A's in green, all E's in yellow, and so on, in my mind. This color system also helped me to recall words and to learn languages easier than others. Vowels colored every syllable correctly for me, even when heard. And once I recalled the color of a word, the word itself was then remembered by me. I often wondered if schools everywhere should use this simple system. Interestingly enough, my sister saw vowels in different colors from mine, so Herr Nagel must have used different crayons when he taught her to write vowels.

Mother's parents had moved in with us several years ago. World War I had closed all of grandfather's factories in foreign lands, and everything was appropriated by the various governments. The galloping inflation in Germany then had taken the last of their funds. I remember with awe that whenever Aunt Annie visited us, the two math geniuses (she and her father) walked around in the garden and played serious games of chess, without a chessboard in sight! I was always amazed that none of us three children inherited their talents.

In the spring of 1931 grandfather died. He had been ill for some time. I remember his death so vividly because I saw a human body for the first time.

My parents knew he was dying, and they sent us children with one of the maids into the forest, where we picked bouquets of snow-white anemones, which carpeted

Mother's father, Dr. Phil. Hans Leffler, about 1927

35

the forest floor every spring. When we came home with our flowers we were led upstairs to his bright little room, where one could look down directly onto our spring-blossomed fruit trees and across the entire village. And there grandfather lay on his bed—white, quiet, peaceful as if asleep. We placed our flowers into his hands, which were folded in prayer. And none of us cried, because we assumed he was in heaven now.

Father had long managed to talk the village into clearing the badly neglected little cemetery behind the schoolhouse. And he made them erect a wall of brick to keep out the pigs and chickens. Grandfather was buried there, at the back of the cemetery in a corner by the wall. Father erected a large wooden cross with grandfather's name initialed on it. This was to become our family burial plot, but Germany had other plans for us and for millions of families...

In the spring of 1932 Father decided to accept one of two positions he was offered in Berlin. One parish was in the wealthy area west of Berlin, the other in the east, which was much poorer and quite drab. And, of course, Father chose the east.

A week ahead of the move we children were bundled off to Mother's brother, Uncle Engbert, in Kassel. He resided there with his wife and little daughter. He was an engineer in charge of Kassel's waterworks and was a warm, lively, and generous uncle to us.

I suppose we were sent there to spare us (and our parents) a heartbreaking farewell from our maids, our house, and our beloved animals.

My sister told me years later that the villagers' farewell to my parents went as follows: Just before Father left, he had transferred his deed to the Elizabeth Haus to the village! Despite his secrecy about it, word got out. Carloads of farmers and wagonloads of their families arrived at the train station, where my parents were about to board the train to Berlin. There were gifts and flowers and red faces and apologies for their atrocious behavior toward Father all these years. They even pleaded with my parents to change their mind and stay. They had finally realized what an exceptionally great pastor they had had.

When the Nazis appropriated the Elizabeth Haus a few years later, they had to pay the village a large sum of money for it.

The Church of the Good Samaritan in East Berlin

See the Evil

1931 to 1933

Berlin was not even a hundred miles northeast; less than a two-hour train trip. But it might as well have been located light years away on a different planet, as far as I was concerned.

The immensity of this unfathomable sea of tall, gray, tightly pressed together buildings overwhelmed me. And the maze of endless hard streets—with not a tree or a blade of grass on them—confused me, hurt my feet, and offended my sense of beauty. The busy people streaming back and forth, ignoring me or pushing me aside, seemed like hostile aliens. I felt so terribly insignificant and unnecessary.

Thank heaven I had Hans! We clung to each other more closely than ever for comfort and company. We felt like castaways on a storm swept shore.

Of course, slowly the concept of "home" and "neighborhood" became a somewhat more acceptable reality. But I knew that—for the rest of my life—I would never again feel as happy, safe, innocent, important to others and therefore to myself, as I had felt before arriving in Berlin.

East Berlin is, and probably always will be, a blue-collar working-man's sector—functional rather than attractive, with its small owner-run shops offering simple daily necessities. To find the department stores, elegant boutiques, outdoor cafes, tree-lined avenues emerging from huge parks, famous hotels, museums, dome and castle, one had to take the subways, streetcars or "el" to the center of the city, and go west from there. We children were seldom taken in that direction. But in fairness, my parents did not travel there often, either, for much of Father's salary went to the poor of the parish.

The *Samariter Church* ("Church of the Good Samaritan") to which Father had been assigned as one of three clergyman, was on the Samariter Street, diagonally across from our apartment house. It was about as large and high as our village church had been, but here—on an isle surrounded by tall buildings—its size was perfect. It was also of Gothic design, and the main tower was topped with a very tall spire. There was a clock on each side, and the inside of the tower—way up high—held six huge bells. They rang each evening at six o'clock and for every Sunday service. On New Year's Eve they started at midnight and rang for an hour, where they competed with thousands of firecrackers and could still be heard.

Long steps led up to the portal beneath a tall Christ-figure. Inside I loved the stain glass windows best. They depicted the story of the Good Samaritan. The sun filtered through them and filled the entire church with a warm glow.

Inside our church

Behind the church was a small grass plot with a lovely weeping willow. This tree, along with a few geraniums gracing some of the thousands of balconies, were the only reminders of nature. There was just one exception—Father's balcony. There, the trellises he had constructed supported brightly-flowered vines to frame the balcony. And from the boxes cascaded thickly hundreds of peonies of every color and shape. They streamed down the front of the building. Every summer, this balcony was an oasis in the desert.

Owned by the Lutheran Church, the house was stuccoed and painted pitch-black, with huge golden letters along the top spelling *Samariter Haus*. Four stories could be reached by a small, private elevator, to which only the adults had the key, or by a wide spiral staircase. The second and fourth floors were occupied by the other two clergymen, while the third was ours.

Out of Step

I must admit that, despite my despair and anger about our move from the country, I was much impressed with our apartment. It was, I think, the largest, brightest and most interesting big city apartment I have ever seen anywhere, to this day. And it needed to be—if only to accommodate my parents' "open door policy," Hans's and my constant need for exercise, and Odi's insistence on privacy.

Before Berlin, I had loved the outdoors, but now, for the time being at least, the apartment became my haven. It featured a center hall from where one could enter the "salon" and the children's playroom. A hallway led to the entrance and the "waiting room," and on to Father's study. Another hallway went to the bedrooms, and a third one to the guest and kitchen area.

When Father was home he could usually be found in his study. If he needed one of us, he would push a button on his desk: One ring would summon Odi, two for me, and three for Hans. The study was lined with heavy black bookcases, which reached nearly the high ceiling. One side of the room was almost totally occupied by a huge, paper-laden desk. Above it hung an oil painting of Mother in her blue velvet, low-cut dress, with the long golden chain as her only jewelry. Whoever had painted it caught her lovely but serious face and the thoughtful expression in her large dark eyes to perfection.

An immense aquarium filled the space beneath all three windows. All clear and lit, it was a paradise for the many tropical fishes. No one but Father fed them and cleaned the tank. Mother sometimes despaired about water stains on the touchy parquet floor, but we all realized how much this stressed man needed hobbies, and we pooled our meager resources every birthday to buy him another fish.

Our apartment in East Berlin, "House of the Good Samaritan." First floor: Kindergarten; Second floor: Nazi clergy; Third floor: Our apartment; Fourth floor:Nazi clergy; Fifth floor: Medical offices. Today, our apartment houses the Lutheran Synod offices.

Tall double doors led from Father's study to the waiting room. No one ever really waited there, but his assistants had their desk in there, a table was used to crank out Father's weekly newsletter, and the room was usually filled with young and old parishioners, milling or meeting. There, the glass doors led to the flowery balcony, and one corner held my piano. It was called "Gisela's piano," because I had a high, clear soprano singing voice and was therefore mistakenly considered to be musical. To this day, I feel sorry for the young organist who tried to get my clumsy fingers to master Kuhlau etudes. And I feel even sorrier for the assistants, who had to suffer through my efforts for one to two hours daily.

This room became the family room at night. We gathered there mainly to listen to a powerful radio Father had bought in order to catch bits and pieces of the usually jammed news from foreign stations. This was soon punishable by imprisonment, and we took many precautions not to be overheard.

The waiting room was connected to the "salon" by two milk-glass sliding doors, which met in the middle. Here one stepped onto old Persian rugs, and the only light necessary was an opera house-sized chandelier, which fascinated me to no end with its iridescent crystal of square sticks and round baubles. I could reach some of them to make them glitter in rainbow colors and tinkle softly like chimes in the wind.

We also called it the "grand dining room" because the table by the couch could be lengthened to accommodate up to 20 guests. They were served on heavy starched linen with delicate Meissen or Bavarian china. A smaller Biedermeier desk was Mother's private corner. And rows of tiered tropical plants under stain-glass windows were another hobby for Father.

One day when I came home from school I was led into the grand room to find a grand piano in it! A musical great-aunt had died and left it to me! Of course, everyone else was proud of this elegant addition to our household, but I felt more pressured than ever to produce harmony instead of agony. Well, at least my teacher loved it, and occasionally a guest brought it to life.

There was a connecting door to our playroom, but it was barred from that side by our "great toy cabinet," which featured games like chess and backgammon, which I never mastered, along with tools to further creativity such as plywood saws, easels, paints, and knitting needles. One special treasure for Hans and me needed adult assistance—a set of animal molds into which one could pour molten lead to make stand-up animals!

The playroom had another balcony that featured kitchen herbs, tomatoes, cabbages, and the like. And in winter it held spoilable meats and such.

The playroom also doubled as the daily dining room. Here, too, were samples of Father's inventiveness: three high, wooden chairs were initialed "O," "G," and "H." As we grew taller, Father simply sawed off pieces of chair legs to adjust our height to that of the tabletop. Eventually, of course, all three chairs were of normal height.

Out in the center hall stood a white glass cabinet. Most visitors, who hung up their coats in that hall, stared at it in disbelief or even horror. It held wild animals, stuffed and incredibly lifelike. They had not been killed by humans, but had been found lifeless by Father or us in "our" forest. A red, bushy-tailed fox seemed to pounce. Above him, shelves held several species of owls, perched or flying majestically. A raven was headed toward you, and a weasel sprinted away. Farther up, snakes floated in formaldehyde, as well as rare species of frogs. Even a pink and white Mexican axolotl was featured, which is an amphibian capable of breathing under water as well as on land, and had been the subject of Mother's years of research for her doctoral dissertation.

My other memories of this hall consist mainly of laundry being sorted before it was sent out, and of helping Father button down his long, flowing black robes, then reaching him his beret and watching him as he torturously tied the stiffly starched white "bib" behind his neck, which completed the garb for Lutheran officiating.

Many an early morning, as we children were about to hurry to school—usually bleary-eyed, sans breakfast, and in a rotten mood—Father would corral us in this hall for a lengthy morning prayer. I suppose he was imitating his idol, Martin Luther. I stood with bowed head, praying mainly for a quick and merciful end to all these blessings, so I would not have to run all the way. By the way, to this day I feel numb and exhausted mornings. As the afternoon progresses, so does my energy. Obviously my biological clock is simply not in time with the rest of humanity. I noticed with glee, though, that Mother and Odi had a similar problem.

From here, the hallway leading to the bedrooms featured wooden shelves built by Father to accommodate preserves. Cherries and elderberries were sometimes boiled by Mother with cornstarch added, to provide a cool "soup" for summer eves. I remember vividly staring at the little white worms in the cherry soups of a bad crop. I gagged but I ate it, for "wasting God's food is a sin!" and Mother was watching us closely. Much later—when all Berlin was

starving—worse things were contained among the last preserves, such as jams made 90% of rotten carrots, and believe it or not, crow meat became dinner! It looked very
bad and tasted even worse.

But I am digressing again…

Then came our children's bedroom, which became my
very own room when I turned nine. It was almost as big as
the salon, but was just right for three beds and night tables
and for a long row of wardrobes placed side by side, which
served the whole family. Built-in closets were unknown in
those days.

Hans and I used the adjoining tops to create a miniature zoo, complete with homemade cages, parks, pens, and
even a pool for the seals. There was a host of exotic animals, consisting of the ones we formed from lead and gifts
from adults. No one bothered us up there. We used stacked
chairs to clamber up.

This children's bedroom also holds vivid memories of
Grandmother taking turns sitting by each bed at night, telling us wonderful tales about her childhood adventures. She
often yielded to our pleas of "More!" until Mother appeared
in the doorway. Grandmother also snuck us a piece of candy
occasionally, as a "little bed hopper."

A door connected our room to that of our parents.
There, to me, the most impressive object was a large, black-
and-white picture above the simple metal double bed. It
showed a wild, stormy sea. A fully clothed man and woman
stood in the surf holding hands and looking serenely toward shore, as the waves jumped foaming against their
clothes, and the storm tore at them. Even at my young age
I understood the meaning of this picture.

Even the small mirrored anteroom to the bath holds
memories for me, such as Mother singing her curls with

the glowing iron when we broke her concentration. Or my strictly forbidden attempts at putting on make-up when the parents were out. But most of all my desperate tries to make my hated pigtails look somewhat more attractive. It was not permitted to cut or even to unwind them.

On the right of that hallway was yet one more room. It became Odi's hideaway which she only had to share when Grandmother spent some winter months with us.

It faced an ugly backyard, so the drapes were usually drawn. Over the couch hung an oil portrait of Grandmother as a young girl. It was life-size, showing Grandmother as a young woman in a black, high-neck lace gown, blond ringlets covering her forehead above grey eyes and small, slender hands languidly in her lap holding a white flower.

Hans and I were only allowed in Odi's sanctuary if we knocked and she granted permission. We did not knock frequently, but when we did we found her usually painting, sewing, reading, or doing homework, and hating to be disturbed. She was growing tall rapidly now at age 10 and 11. (I never grew much until I was about 12, but then I also made it to 5' 9"). Her hair was raven-black and shiny, while mine was "only brown." Her teeth were gleaming-white and pearly-perfect, while mine had a space in front and were of ivory color. And her eyes were a deep-brown versus my grey ones. What angered me most was the heart shape of her face, while mine was square. Only my nose seemed better proportioned.

Needless to say, I spent years of agony thinking of myself as the ugly duckling in this beautiful family. But eventually even my sister had to concede that I had become pretty. And then we finally became friends. As children, though, she loathed Hans's and my immaturity, loudness, and togetherness; we resented her harsh criticism, snobbishness, and alignment with adults. We avoided one another like the plague.

The third hallway led mainly to the kitchen, but on its way passed by a small guestroom with its own bath. Here Father's assistants slept occasionally, especially when we children were away on vacation. They were usually single, bright and tolerant young men. They had finished all theological studies and passed their final exams and were clergymen. But they had to assist a pastor for a year before they were allowed to officiate at weddings and other "official" occasions. They preached in Father's absence. Every one of them showed courage simply by working for Father. It automatically made them "an enemy of the Reich" as Father was labeled by the Nazis, and put them in grave danger. But more about all this later.

When Hans got the room he spent little time in there, especially since his desk was mainly meant for homework, which he loathed.

We now arrive in the immense kitchen, walls tiled in grey with a border of Dutch windmills and rural scenes. The large stove had once been coal-fired, but now was gas. A steep spiral staircase led from there to the backyard and cellar, in case of fire. And a larder held buckets of cold water to keep milk, butter and eggs from spoiling. Meats and fish had to be purchased daily and parfried or parboiled immediately to keep from spoiling. Without refrigeration or even fans of any kind, summers in that baking city were something of a nightmare, which we escaped at every opportunity.

Hans and I used the ledge of the china cabinet in the kitchen to make ourselves big, open-faced sandwiches nightly, consisting of dark rye covered with lard. We also snuck quarts of fresh lemonade to bed. We two were always hungry. I am sure our parents knew about these kitchen raids, but they barely commented. Probably because other family members—including Mother herself—helped themselves at times. For Mother was a total failure as a cook! Dinners consisted mainly of unpeeled boiled potatoes, awash with boiled, pureed spinach or cabbage, which was served warmed-over three to four days in a row. An occasional piece of tough, boiled, cow meat, a burned fried egg or hamburger, or—goodie—a boiled, waterlogged, totally tasteless piece of sea fish floated in the spinach or cabbage. Luckily, Hans and I adored potatoes in any form, especially if they were re-fried for supper. But Odi was not so lucky—she detested even the potatoes. So eventually, in sheer self-defense, she learned to cook and served us a more varied diet, such as pancakes, salads and noodles.

Another larder—this one for dry foods—adjoined Hans's bath. Sometimes mice found their way into it. We did not kill them, but used baited cages which let the mice get in but not out again. Then we transported them to the street and set them free via a small door in the cage.

Above this second larder in the hallway was a crawl space, just high and long enough to allow Hans and me to furnish it with pillows and blankets to make it "our house." What a sanctuary! It took a stepladder to get into it, and we pulled that up after us to be undisturbed. Only one other person was allowed up there, and that was Hans's loyal little friend, Berthold. I soon realized I needed to overcome my immediate jealousy if I wanted to keep my brother's friendship. So the three of us became an almost inseparable trio. We used the crawlspace to play Father (Hans), Mother (me), and son (Berthold). We "parents" helped Berthold (who was a very lazy scholar) to learn reading, writing and so on, and read him the Grimm's fairytales we so loved.

We carried little meals up there and served them to each other on Odi's former doll's china.

Berthold was the son of a neighboring policeman and his tired wife. They were happy to have their son spending most of his time in our company, rather than that of the mainly unsavory neighborhood kids. And our parents were glad that Berthold helped us to adjust to city life, for despite his small stature, he was quite wise already to the ways of the neighborhood kids and prevented Hans and me from making the wrong acquaintances.

We three were also allowed to play cowboys and Indians in the playroom. We fashioned ourselves a teepee, consisting of a tablecloth donated by Mother for that purpose. We fastened the top to the top of the toy cabinet, and the bottom onto the playroom floor, which was covered with maltreated linoleum. We made ourselves feathered headdresses (the feathers were donated by a pillow shop, which used Eider down), tomahawks, and bows and arrows. And then we imitated the fascinating American Indian stories as written by Karl Mai, which were all the rage of German youngsters in those days. Although the author had never been to America himself, his portrayals of a great chief he called Winnetou—along with Winnetou's friend, the pioneer Old Shatterhand—and their fascinating adventures filled many books, beautifully illustrated in color. They aroused in us a deep longing for the wilderness of America.

One side of the ugly backyard of our apartment house featured the great parish hall, which was used for parish get-togethers, Bible hours, the church youth orchestra, guest speakers, or for Father showing slides about the Bible or Martin Luther. Every Wednesday evening Father led the Bible hour down there, with Mother in attendance. Berthold was supposed to be home by then, and we were to be engrossed in homework. But on Wednesday, as soon as my parents had departed, we let Berthold back into our apartment. Odi was told to keep our secret under threat of bodily injury from the three of us. We felt totally safe from discovery, because we could hear the last hymn being sung downstairs, which gave us time to send Berthold home and straighten up the place. But twice we were so engrossed in play that we forgot to pay attention to that final hymn.

Here's what happened the first time. We heard the key in the front door. What to do with Berthold?! We ran panic-stricken toward my room, since it was farthest away from the entrance, but my bed was too low for pudgy Berthold to crawl under. Then I happened to look at the oversized laundry hamper. We stuffed him in there and slammed the lid shut, just as Mother entered the room to hang up her coat into one of the "zoo" wardrobes. But our sigh of relief stopped dead as she next headed for the laundry hamper to deposit a hankie, and promptly pulled Berthold up by his scruffy hair…

The second time was even worse. At the sound of the front door key, Berthold hid successfully and sneaked out when he had a chance. But we had just cooked ourselves baking chocolate with sugar and cleaned up the mess and opened the window. What to do with the still runny chocolate? Again we ran for my room and deposited the pan onto a top shelf in a wardrobe. Lo and behold, Mother entered and went directly to that very cabinet, opened it, and tried to put her hat on the shelf! Down came the pan of still quite warm chocolate, smack onto Mother's head, with a flood of chocolate streaming down her hair and face onto the lily-white blouse of her suit! Mother wrote later in her memoirs, "and we all laughed heartily." But I clearly remember a drastically different ending!

One thing the whole family was sure of—namely, that Mother had the gift of ESP.

Hans, Odi, and I were now unhappy students in the elementary school, located just three blocks downhill in one of those endless grey side streets. The school was even uglier than the apartment houses among which it squatted. And the tiny, walled-in schoolyard resembled that of a prison. There we were herded during breaks, and walked around in a tight circle, munching our sandwiches and being watched every second by a teacher.

My village curriculum was not considered to be sufficient here, and I was forced to repeat a school year. I never did become a very good student in German schools. They had always bordered on the military throughout their history. Teachers were God, and you were nothing. I hated and dreaded every school day, and my thoughts were mainly on the upcoming vacations.

One of the few things I liked in this school was the annual play. I was usually awarded a starring role, but never a feminine one, of course, which was fine with me. Two plays stand out in my mind rather vividly. In the first one I was the big bad wolf in *Little Red Riding Hood*. The heroine was a classmate I had befriended somewhat, the chubby, white-and-pink Eva. On the day of the play, Mother had finally let me buy the ultra-realistic wolf's mask, which I had long discovered in a small shop. No one had seen it yet, and when I suddenly appeared on stage, Little Red Riding Hood let out a piercing shriek and fainted! I kid you not—she actually hit the stage floor! She never forgave me, of course, and neither did her parents who were in the audience. And what happened to the play? Well, it sort of dragged on from there with a substitute for Eva, and I played my role well enough, but minus the mask.

A year later I was the king who had a giant golden key (made of cardboard) dangling from a chain around his waist, because only the king himself could open the three doors to his three daughters for the right suitors. I got so carried away with my role of the powerful king that I rammed the key with all my might against door number one when I was supposed to unlock it. Not only did the door cave in to reveal the stunned number one daughter, but my cardboard key broke in half, to the awful sound of the audience roaring with laughter! The agony dragged on, of course, because I wore that ugly stump around my waist 'til the end of the play, and had to open doors number two and three with it yet, with the audience breaking up every time.

But school soon became unimportant to me. That year—and especially the winter—of 1932 Berlin experienced its worst joblessness and depression. This was, of course, one of the reasons why it was fairly easy for Hitler to grab the power. Many Germans saw him as the savior from misery and shame. The shame most Germans felt should have been about the Germans starting World War I, but they felt shame only because they lost it!

Father, of course, could not stand idly by while so many people around us were jobless and starving. So he admonished those parishioners who still had jobs to help feed the hungry. They responded, and with their help he rented an empty store with a small kitchen, just around the corner from our Samariter Haus. He named it *Heim* (home), and it soon became just that to about 12 homeless men. And now the wealthy merchants, wholesalers and bankers from every part of Berlin got to know my father. He begged, wheedled, threatened, beguiled and moved the rich to donations of food, coal, cloth, money, toys, you name it. Then

The homeless employed by Father at the "Heim"

he opened a soup kitchen in the Heim, where his homeless dozen and some parish women now cooked and served at first several hundred, and eventually 1,500 dinners per day. People stood in long lines outside, but were served quickly. Most took the food home. They paid one nickel per portion! We children often accompanied some of the 12 on an old cart with an old horse, donated by someone. We loaded it with the donated fruits, vegetables and meats from the softened-up wholesalers, along with coal from Berlin's huge coal yards, to heat the Heim and the homes of the jobless.

Father made sure each one of the 12 learned a trade or practiced their own trade. So the Heim now sported a carpenter, several tailors and cooks, a shoemaker, painter, and even a toymaker! They worked with all the donated materials and it all then went to the needy.

The parish had been nearly dormant when Father first started there. The other two clergymen—elderly, conservative and lazy—had badly neglected their duty. Father tried valiantly at first to get along with them, but it was fruitless: they hated him even before he arrived. They were especially furious when he opened the Heim, and they openly made fun of him and called him the "rags pastor." They were very worried about Father's rising popularity, as their own congregations dwindled.

After Hitler took over, those two "wolves-in-sheep-skins" were among the first people on the street to fly the Nazi flag from their balconies above and below us. Father flew the old black, white, and red striped flag defiantly. This was forbidden, of course, and these two (abbreviated from now on as K and H) denounced us immediately to the party. When Father was then threatened with imprisonment he rolled up the flag and never flew any.

Soon the Nazis took over every institution in the country. One of the first they tried to destroy was the Lutheran Church, to make it into a propaganda tool for the Third Reich. In 1933 they already had simply dismissed the residing bishop and made a Nazi puppet the infamous *Reichsbishop*. His name was Müller, and his edicts were to become church law. One of the first things he did was to discourage the teaching of the Old Testament, because that was a "Jewish book"! All Nazi ministers under his guidance now called themselves German Christians (*Deutsche Christen*, or DC for short). Very soon the great majority of German Lutheran clergy became DC members!

But a small minority of resisters now grew as the horror of the Nazi regime became more and more apparent. One hundred Berlin pastors met secretly in a suburb of Berlin, and 99 of them formed the Confessing Church (*Bekennende Kirche*, or BK for short). (The one hundredth pastor had to go home first "to ask his wife's permission."

He later joined, too). And the 99—Father among them, of course—named Dr. Martin Niemöller as the head of the BK.

Dr. Martin Niemöller, by the way, became the hero of us all. Not only was he a profound world-renowned theologian, but he was an example of courage and leadership in the church's struggle against a vicious dictator. He was a powerful voice of conscience for mankind.

Father told us that Hitler had asked Niemöller to meet with him and explain the church's resistance to him. After that discussion Hitler hated him more than ever.

The Nazi-resisting clergymen formed a nationwide association. Loosely translated it was called the Pastors' Emergency Fellowship. Members addressed each other as "Brother," such as "Brother Harnisch." I remember one evening when I was about ten years old, how proud we three children were that Father was closeted with Niemöller and some other Brothers in his study, and how we whispered and tiptoed in order not to disturb them.

Once I heard Dr. Niemöller speak to an overflow audience at his church in Berlin-Dahlem (a western suburb) where he and his family lived. It was a biblically-based, powerful call to resist evil, and he was arrested again shortly thereafter.

When I was about eleven I decided to make him a Christmas present to show him my admiration and gratitude. I copied his picture from one of his book jackets onto a piece of plywood. Then I sawed it out, painted it black, lacquered it, pasted this silhouette on a white background, sawed a frame for it and glued everything together. On the back of the picture I wished him a merry Christmas and signed it, "From your admirer Gisela Harnisch." Odi, of course, did not think it was artistic enough, but my parents thought it looked fine. Father gave it to Dr. Niemöller and reported back to me that he thanked me very much, saying he would hang it above his desk.

And so, Father came home from the BK meeting and assembled us all in the hall, telling us what he had done. Then he added, "I have now entrusted all our lives solely into the hands of the Lord." We children did not realize yet what this meant, but Mother trembled, though she fully agreed that we must now become "outlaws of conscience."

The Labyrinth

1934 to 1936

A t this young age I did not really understand the details of the church's struggle in general or Father's in particular. But I personally started to feel the oppression quite drastically, along with my parents' admirable attempts to relieve some of the stress for us children.

German teachers were always in the forefront of those professionals who changed political allegiances as fast as a chameleon changes its colors to protect itself. In my own lifetime I knew them as hearty fans of the emperor, then as adorers of Hitler, followed by their ardent communism, and finally by their unquestioned acceptance of capitalism. Yet they, too, had their small minority of thinkers and resisters who endured bravely the ostracism, ridicule, denunciations from fellow teachers or students, license removals, or even prison in the days of the Third Reich.

We had one such teacher in the elementary school. His first name was Klaus, but I never addressed him as such in school. He was especially incensed by the fact that the Nazis had immediately outlawed all youth organizations except their own. These were the infamous Hitler youth groups, the HJ for boys and the BDM (*Bund Deutscher Mädchen*) for girls, which every youngster was told to join. These were, of course, paramilitary Nazi units steeped in propaganda and led by older, fanatic party members who encouraged the children to snitch even on their own parents if they criticized the Führer. Because all German children had suffered frequent corporal punishment at home (including we three), the Nazi youth groups now gave the kids a chance to seek revenge on adults. Many a parent and other kinfolk went to prison because of totally false accusations by their own children.

Klaus was a rebel, like Father, and decided to start a traditional *Wandervögel* (Roving Birds) group in defiance of the Nazi ban. He met with my parents and they then allowed Odi and myself to join this secret youth group. Hans was too young yet.

We met evenings with older *Wandervögel* and Klaus at a secret location, weekly. There we sang the old folksongs that Klaus taught us. Some were so rare they had never been published in songbooks, but had been kept alive by *Wandervögel* throughout history. I memorized them and noted them down at home. Klaus accompanied our singing on his guitar, as did several other *Wandervögel*. There we also planned our occasional nature hikes, which I particularly loved. These took place on several weekends, come rain or shine. About 20 of us would leave by train, knapsacks on our backs. We spread out into different compartments and cars so as not to be recognized by the Nazis as a group. And then we met in the heather areas, northwest of Berlin toward Hamburg. Oh, the purple stretches of heather as far as the eye could see. They were interspersed with stands of delicate white birches, and single, dark-green junipers, pointing like fingers

The outlawed "Roving Birds" hiking in northern Germany. Gisela is in front.

to the blue summer sky. Flaming-yellow gorse bushes lent even more color to the scenery. And there was innocent, busy life all around us, too: honey bees and rabbits and little green lizards; even an occasional herd of white sheep. We hiked and sang about the heather and about old mills. And especially about a secret blue flower which *Wandervögel* had always attempted to find…

Odi soon tired of all this physical exertion and quit the group. But I relished every minute of it all. I was by far the youngest of the "roving birds." They made me feel accepted, protected and loved. I kept up with them all, too, in those many hours of uninterrupted hiking, and I sang my heart out. At night we arrived bushed at some farm, where we were allowed to sleep in the hayloft of the barn. There, even though I could hardly keep my eyes open any longer, I did not want to miss a single word of Klaus's ghost stories about the heather and moors, which got scarier and scarier until we begged for mercy.

After less than a year someone must have gotten careless and talked, because the Nazis discovered our existence. Klaus called my parents quickly—it was all over. I never saw him again, and he never showed up for teaching in the fall. I suppose the Nazis had revoked his license, or worse.

In 1935 I was 10 and had passed the entrance exams for a college-prep school for girls, the lyzeum. I was to attend in the fall. One day in June there came a phone call to my parents from a music teacher I had before she quit the year before. She told my parents that she had been hired as the director of the famous German Children's Choir, which consisted of the best voices of Berlin. The choir was part of the German broadcasting system, located in a western suburb of Berlin. I knew where that was, because the tower, called the *Funkturm,* was famous, and even featured a café with a tremendous view of the city near its top. Well, Miss Z then explained to my parents that she had been impressed with my high and clear soprano voice when I was in her class, and she wanted me for that choir! To my amazement and happiness my parents consented!

Mother accompanied me there for my first trip so I could learn how to use the complicated subways and "els." Then I was on my own. In the beginning I was almost nauseous with excitement and tension. But my young and beautiful Miss Z managed to relax me in our practice sessions. And what a wondrous world of which I now became a part: silent elevators without doors went slowly up and down past each of the many floors (you had to step alertly in and out of them!). The hallways were plushly carpeted, and so were all the broadcasting rooms and stages, to minimize noise. Red lights on the outside of the rooms indicated if there was a broadcast happening inside. Huge clocks everywhere, monitors behind glass screens, "noise makers" for door imitations, and thunder and such. Musicians dragging their bass fiddles behind them along the hallways. And even movie stars sometimes coming towards me, with chattering entourages following them. I got their autographs, or if they were rushed they sometimes just petted my head! But even more excitement was in store for me. Miss Z, after just a few practice sessions, decided I and another (older) girl should be the soloists of the choir! Now my cup truly ran over! And then started the weekly live broadcasts, where I heard myself sing, as in a dream. Sometimes softly for the lullaby solos, sometimes my voice powerfully leading the choir, which echoed the part I sang. And always the violins of the famous huge Berlin orchestra engulfing and carrying me. Few mishaps happened, but one of them occurred while we were luckily being taped rather than live. I had not eaten all day and slept little, and my hectic lifestyle caught up with my rather sensitive *vasovagal* system—I passed out just before my solo. Thank god for the plush rugs and for my fellow soloist.

I gladly gave up my planned summer vacation. I even got paid, and my parents received the checks. I was so proud to be able to contribute to the scarce family income. My family, of course, always listened to my weekly evening broadcasts. I remember my proud Father sometimes happily limping through the apartment while imitating my voice and songs 'til we all laughed tears. Our parishioners, too, listened to the pastor's daughter and I was fast becoming a little celebrity, especially in the fall when school started. Then suddenly—after a year or so—it was all over.

The Nazis had gotten around to insisting that this radio choir had to wear the BDM uniforms, especially for all photo sessions for publicity. My parents tried not to influence me. I am sure the family and the whole parish would have forgiven me had I decided to join the Hitler Youth in order to save my budding stardom. But I refused to wear that uniform and was therefore fired on the spot. None of us ever listened to that choir again, and despite my hurt I felt proud to have become an active member of the resistance martyrs.

All through my school years my refusal to wear that uniform caused me no end of trouble, culminating eventually in the fact that I was not allowed to graduate, and was therewith barred from any German university (which frankly did not bother me one bit then). My grades throughout my schooling were very mediocre and a joke—the Nazi teachers gave me nothing but C's and D's, even in my most favored subjects such as literature, creative writing and history. And an occasional Nazi resister would give me A's in subjects I hated, such as art, sewing, French, and even geometry or chemistry! I always feared school, but could never take it seriously. And daydreaming about vacations away from Berlin became almost an obsession with me. Some of these dreams became a reality.

Father decided to buy a used boat when I was nine. He never had time for lengthy vacations, and a boat in and near Berlin would let him "get away from it all" at least occasionally.

The Spree and the Havel are the two rivers that crisscross Berlin. They form many lovely lakes ringing the city. And farther out yet they fill long peaceful coves within the tall conifer forests.

The boat on the Spree River (Berlin)

I am sure that several concerned relatives of Father's—
who were all better off financially than we were—helped
pay for the boat and its mooring and storing fees at the
nearest yacht club. It was a rather odd-looking vessel, sort
of a cross between an outboard motorboat and a cabin
cruiser. The cabin accommodated three for sleeping, but
the few times all five of us slept on the boat in the same
night, Hans and I ended up in the open part of the boat,
stung by mosquitoes and even rained on. But not to worry;
Father designed and had a high wooden canopy built from
which heavy tarps unfurled at night, fastened tightly to
the rim of the boat. It worked, except that a narrow boat
with a high superstructure becomes tippy. We nearly capsized several times on trips when a wind came up and
roused the waves on one of the big lakes. It certainly was
not transportation for someone prone to seasickness.

Whenever we had a chance, Hans and I walked an hour
to the yacht club where the boat was moored during off-
season. If the water was not too cold, we dove into it from
the pier and swam about one and a half miles to a little
unoccupied island, where we pretended to be shipwrecked

or staged treasure hunts. The water in this small inner-city lake was oily and dirty from the factories surrounding it, including the mighty Siemens works, where my uncle Alexander was an engineer. And many tourist steamboats crisscrossed the little lake on weekends. But none of this deterred Hans and me from swimming on and on.

For the summer we finally all got together for one weekend to make "the great boat trip to distant shores," with Father steering it as the proud captain. Hans and I spent most of the day-long trip sitting on top of the cabin, with swimsuits on in case we fell in. We sat as much forward as one possibly could, watching the bow cutting through the water, dangling our feet into the spray, our seafaring songs competing with the cries of the seagulls that followed us everywhere.

We anchored most summers in one of those lovely long coves, not too far from a little village. We had a canoe, too, which was tied alongside the boat for the trip, and served to get to the village to pick up family members or groceries and kerosene.

We three children were often all alone out there. But since there was no criminal activity anywhere we feared nothing. We even got along with Odi pretty well then. The evenings were the best, when the sun set and the nightlife came alive, the fog setting in and the call of the loons. We read Karl Mai and Grimm's fairytales by the light of a kerosene lamp that swung back and forth with the wave movements of the boat. Only lightning was dangerous on the water, and we felt an electric surge when a tree was struck nearby.

Hans and I used the canoe often for our excursions, and we were dismayed when one day our assistant pastor showed up. He slept in the village inn, and Father gave him sole use of the canoe during the days. Hans and I were not particularly fond of that year's assistant, anyway. His name was Pastor N and he was fat and homely. He always peered at Hans and me through the thick lenses of his glasses with distaste, because we were too noisy around the apartment for his liking. At any rate, Hans and I simmered with anger about the loss of our beloved canoe to this intruder.

Hans, age 8 (1935)

We saw our chance when he had to spend a Sunday in the city to preach for Father who was on the boat with us. We waited until our parents napped in the cabin and Odi was sketching trees again. Then we silently untied the canoe from the boat, ignoring all of Pastor N's belongings in it such as pillows, sunglasses, magazines and all. We paddled to the opposite shore and finally espied something of interest: a cage with two raccoons in it. The problem was that on the long pier a sign was posted saying, PRIVATE PROPERTY: TRESPASSERS WILL BE PROSECUTED. We decided that feeding pastor N's cookies to the coons was worth the risk. We tied the canoe to the pier and tiptoed to the cages. Then we heard a noise in the underbrush...panic-stricken we raced back to the canoe, untied it and jumped into it, forgetting that one must get into a canoe very, very carefully. We found ourselves immediately under the capsized canoe, while our heavy woolen gym suits and shoes dragged us down. Somehow we managed to surface. We even managed to bail enough so the canoe would not sink, and we retrieved our floating-away paddles. But Pastor N's entire gear had hopelessly sunk from view, while in reality no one had pursued us!

We got spanked when we got back, but not as hard as we had feared, because all were relieved that we had not drowned (though Hans and I were pretty sure that Pastor N would not have minded much if we had not survived).

Hans & Gisela on the pier

Despite our long feud, we actually made peace with Pastor N one day a few weeks later. He had, as usual, ascended the spiral staircase to the Samariter church's spire in the evening, in order to take the Lutheran Church flag inside for the night. Members of the Hitler youth followed him silently, and when he descended they beat him mercilessly, breaking his nose and several ribs as they pushed him down the staircase. They even stomped on his glasses, too. And yet, Pastor N resumed his duties at Father's side as soon as he was able to walk again! It reminded me of Ada's bravery with the nasty horse, Fritz. Hans and I had learned a valuable lesson—never judge a book by its cover!

We had learned to swim the summer before we got the boat. Hans and I had been sent to Brieg, a small town near the Polish border on the Oder River. There, Grandmother and her unmarried sister Agnes lived in the house which Aunt Agnes had inherited from their parents, and which, by the way, was the locale of so many of Grandmother's bedtime stories to us.

We begged the two ladies to allow us to take swimming lessons in the Oder. They finally gave in, though it was a long walk for them to take us to the river. There, a wooden "swim gym" built directly into the river was the place where kids from miles around learned to swim: first, in the shallower enclosures through which the Oder flowed, and then in the river itself. After just a few exercises with me, the burly middle-aged swim teacher tied a rope around my waist and pushed me into the river—with not a word of warning. I thought I would never make it back up to the surface, because no one took up the slack on the rope. But I made it back up to the top on my own, and since still no one tightened the rope I began to swim. To my amazement I did not drown; I was really swimming!

I made sure no one taught Hans the same drastic way. Soon we became total "swim addicts," which is why Father dared to buy the boat the next year.

The German school year has several smaller vacations built into it, including one in the spring and in the fall, probably because we had school on Saturdays, too. And since there was no money in the family budget for travel we were sent on small vacations and for parts of summers to relatives away from Berlin. The absolute favorite destination for Hans and me was always Aunt Oda's (Father's sister) and her husband Richard's "farming estate." This was a huge house and farmyard with many barns and stables and acres of fields (mainly sugar beets) and gardens, and even stands of woods. It included about 100 cows, plow horses as well as coach horses, and teams of oxen and stalls full of pigs, not counting several dogs, barn cats and countless fowl. It was located near Halle, where my parents had studied. The entire village consisted only of three other estates, a small church, and a few houses belonging to the salaried farmhands. Hourly help was quartered in small, neat apartments or rooms directly above the many stables. There was also a village pond with ducks and geese.

Aunt Oda, Father's sister

Despite all this wealth we felt sorry for Aunt Oda. Uncle Richard turned out to be a womanizer and a drinker and he was usually in a foul mood. He ignored his wife but expected her to supervise the entire dairy production and the large household, and to wine and dine him and his drinking and hunting companions. She herself was quite strict with us children, especially with Odi and me. As girls we were expected to help in the kitchen, and I spent many tortured hours learning to sew and embroider under Aunt Oda's strict supervision. I also accompanied her on her rounds of visits to the sick and the old and the needy, because, like Father, she cared greatly about all suffering humanity. She had been a registered nurse before her marriage, and she now doubled as a doctor in places where it was miles to the nearest hospital, and where accidents were frequent.

But several hours a day I was allowed to join Hans in roaming through the stables and making a host of pets. We were not expected to help, but were asked not to be "underfoot." Our favorite time of day was after sunset, when we were allowed to ride the tired and sweaty plow and draft horses bareback and in our swimsuits to the village pond, where we guided the horses as they swam with us to cool off. And then we proudly rode them back to their stalls.

When in the fall the wheat fields stood empty except for bailed straw in huge pyramids, we roamed them with Uncle Richard's favorite hunting dog, a sleek German pointer, and we took turns hiding from him so he could find us in the haystacks.

Some of my most exciting events happened when I begged, and was allowed, to go along on coach trips to pick up guests from the railroad station. I sat outside on top with the driver, and as soon as we were out of Uncle Richard's view the driver handed me the reins! After the original tense moments I caught on soon, watching and adoring the beautifully decked-out carriage horse, black and shiny, and not at all temperamental like Fritz. It responded obediently to every motion of my little hands as it clip-clopped smartly along the cobblestones. No wonder I spent most of my school hours in Berlin daydreaming about vacations.

I had learned how to ride a bike in Beyersdorf, and taught Hans there, also. As soon as we got back to Berlin we wheedled and begged until our parents got us each a bike. There was not enough money for two, but Mother gave me an old one of hers, and luckily a nearby bike shop fixed it up for me for nothing, because the owner was one of Father's loyal parishioners. And then we were off! Whenever the weather and homework allowed we were practicing in front of our house and eventually making long trips to the outskirts of East Berlin. There was hardly any motor traffic, at least not in East Berlin. After all, even our garbage was still picked up in our first years there by immense garbage wagons, pulled by teams of gorgeous Clydesdales. Beer kegs were delivered to the bars in the same fashion.

Now, of course, we did not have to walk to the boat anymore, either! There was a soccer playing field right next to the yacht club, and when there was no game in progress, Hans and I could practice biking around the big oval. We raced at top speed, egging one another on to ride no-handed and to perform feats on and with our bikes that came close to circus quality.

Most vivid of all the memories are those of Christmas in Berlin. As children we spent weeks ahead of time already making gifts for everyone, including all our relatives. They were simple things, especially since Hans and I were not very handy with saws, beads, crayons, paints and glues. But with Odi's guidance we managed to create crèche figures, Christmas tree decorations, transparents of church windows, or wooden painted angels and Santas.

For four Sundays before Christmas a candle was added to the Advent wreath on the dining table. Then, two weeks before Christmas, Father himself took us to an outdoor Christmas Fair, held every year in the center of Berlin. There were hundreds of brightly-lit booths, offering for sale everything from honey cakes, glazed apples, hot toddies, toys and winter clothing to Christmas trees. Salvation Army solicitors rang bells, toy trains raced around electric tracks, and right in the center the snowflakes whirled around the equally fast whirling horses of a merry-go-round! Even this ugly city had its glorious moments.

Father also started an annual tradition for the congregation. At 5:00 PM on Christmas Eve our Samariter Church became the scene for a children's play, directed by Father and recreating the story of Bethlehem. Odi always portrayed Mary, Hans was one of the three wise men, and I was the angel who carried the star of Bethlehem ahead of the wise men. Since some of the parents could not afford costumes for their children, Mother improvised some at the last minute. She sometimes took the gold-tasseled cloth off the grand piano and fastened it around a wise man. Or she raided our white nightgowns for angel robes. I remember one of the three kings getting our antique brass spittoon pressed onto his head as a very attractive crown.

A carpenter had made a stable and crib in front of the altar. The church was decorated with pine branches and tall, real candles lit the entire church. The players were assembled around the stable, the congregation was finishing a carol, and I was now to lead the three wise men from the vestibule down the aisle to the altar. I held the star of Bethlehem—tied to a broomstick and lit by a bulb inside like a jack-o'-lantern. But suddenly my battery button did not work right, or the wire was loose: The star flickered and went dark most of the trip, and also after I held it above the stable. As I was struggling with the battery I smelled smoke. A little angel next to me had backed up too closely to one of the candles on the altar, and her wings were catching fire. I dropped the star behind the stable, snatched the cape off a nearby shepherd and suffocated the angel's flames before she knew what hit her. Then I grabbed my broomstick and continued my battle with the star-light. It all had happened so quickly that no one noticed it in the audience, and the play went on without interruption.

At the end I was supposed to lead the entire cast back up the aisle to the vestibule. But somehow I had misunderstood Father's directions. I led the parade instead through a side door near the altar and out onto the snowy sidewalk. Like good Germans are wont to do, they all followed me obediently and without thinking through the deep snow along the side of the church 'til we reached the steps, and then the vestibule, where horrified parents were expecting us, and tugging now the sopping wet socks off their shivering little angels. Needless to say, future performances went a lot smoother.

In Germany, presents are exchanged on Christmas Eve already, and we hurried home after the play and waited impatiently for Father to get back from the church. The milk-glass doors to the "salon"—which had been locked to us children for days already—were slowly brightening as we watched them from the hall. All the while we were reciting the biblical Christmas story to Father, in unison, word by word, and from memory. Then the door opened and Mother beckoned us in to gaze in wonder at the glorious tree, which always reached all the way to the ceiling. Dozens of real candles shone unto metal tinsel and unto innumerable glittering ornaments in all colors and forms. There were glass-blown brilliant birds-of-paradise with their long, split tails of spun glass, and colored glass horses, Santas and angels, all with silky hair. Dozens of chocolate stars, gingerbread people, almond cookies, colored sugar rings, gilded walnuts, chocolate toys and music instruments covered with tinfoil of gold and silver, pointed glass icicles, and ornament balls with Christmas scenes inside were just some of the wondrous things on that tree.

My gifts were always on top of my grand piano. They were few, but greatly treasured. And Grandmother's gifts were by the couch, where there stood every year a huge fresh bottle of vermouth. It was about four feet high and a steady source of embarrassment to Grandmother, who loved vermouth but always assured us it was only "for medicinal purposes." We all grinned as we helped her to carry it to her room. She managed to get it empty come spring, and then we took it to the boat for fresh water supplies.

We even got a nice supper then, consisting of our favorite "party" food: potato salad and hot dogs. And on Christmas Day we had a roast goose for dinner, sent to us by Aunt Oda. Only my sister Odi was never able to eat much of that goose: She spent every Christmas night reading a new book while sitting on the floor next to the tree, munching steadily those goodies hanging above her. She was traditionally tired and sick to her stomach on Christmas Day.

In the meantime, pastors K and H continued to make trouble. They denounced Father to their own congregations as a BK member and therefore a "traitor to church and fatherland." They and other DC members urged Reichbishop Müller and his satellites to impeach Father, or at least to transfer him to another parish. They sent young spies into his confirmation class, who then claimed he had maligned the Führer. The first of many Gestapo (Nazi secret police) interrogations of Father began, and finally an arrest and time in jail followed. When Father was picked up for the first time by the "Green Minna" (the jail transport) in front of our house, pastors K and H stood among the spectators and said audibly, "Good riddance!" We all stood on the balcony and cried. Father was released after a few days because of pressure from the BK of Berlin and from his own parishioners.

Soon afterwards an interesting situation developed. A BK member of our congregation was fixing some wiring in our cellar one evening, when he heard K and H's voices among others from behind a locked door. Father investigated the next morning, taking a locksmith with him, who opened the door. Lo and behold, two rooms and a small toilet appeared, complete with a bar and alcoholic spirits. These were obviously boozing rooms for K and H and their buddies. There were evidently women guests, too, because the walls had many slogans praising the female flesh as well as booze. Father had a photographer take detailed photos of the place and sent those to the high church instances of the DC, threatening to disclose everything to the congregations of K and H if they were not immediately relieved of their duties.

And so these two Nazi-no-goods were suddenly gone. We heard that H several months later had died of a heart attack, while K disappeared from anyone's view altogether.

Now the DC installed one new pastor instead of two. He looked like Count Dracula himself, and resembled him in evilness. Pastor U took the apartment below us. He probably later often wished he hadn't, because this gave Hans and me a chance for revenge. Whenever we suspected Pastor U had had a hand in the latest persecutions of Father, Hans and I strung a rope in the hallway by Father's study. Then we took a good run and high-jumped by the hour!

When I was 10, the Nazis suddenly barred Father from access to his own church. But he would not be silenced. Several backrooms in the Heim had in the meantime been let cheaply to several old and poor parish members, but the big front hall was still vacant. So Father turned that into his church. It was scrubbed and painted, with Psalm verses gracing the walls. One end held an altar now, and Father sent out his weekly newsletter to his parishioners that Sunday services would be held there from now on, and he explained why. That first Sunday, both services were overflowing with worshipers as a sign of solidarity with their pastor, which put them all at risk, too, of course. We were very moved. And the louder the Hitler youth paraded and trumpeted in front of the Heim during services to interrupt, the louder we all sang, and the louder Father's voice boomed as he preached.

The parish defied the Nazis in many little ways, and when October 9 came, namely Father's birthday, there was such a sea of flowers and gifts that we had to rent a hall every birthday to accommodate the crowds and speakers and gifts from all over Berlin.

About two years after barring Father from the Samariter Church, the Nazis just as suddenly gave him and his congregation access to it again.

The BK Nazi-resisting clergy of Berlin met at times in forests in the suburbs so they could not be overheard by the Nazis (photos about 1934).

Father appears in the top and bottom photos.

In the forefront, with hands in his pockets, is Dr. Martin Niemoeller, head of the Lutheran Resistance.

Courage

1934 to 1936

4

The worst years for Nazi persecutions of the BK, and therefore of Father, were from 1933 to 1937. And Berlin was the hotbed of it all. As I have said before, I was too young to understand or to be told much. Yet all of us lived in constant fear of Father being tortured and murdered, and maybe Mother, also. Only after 1945 did their letters and memoirs reveal to me what we children had not been told at the time—in order not to endanger ourselves or our parents by talking. They also kept silent because they did not want to traumatize us more than was inevitable. I feel I must fill in these gaps now, to make some sense of it all.

On 60 different occasions Father was taken from our home to Gestapo headquarters, to be interrogated hours on end. And of course, all these times we never knew if he would be returned to us. Many clergymen never came back to their families!

I did not know then, either, that Father had been elected by the high council of the BK to be their liaison to the press. That is, he was to inform the Nazi press of all official BK decisions, and he was also to collect for the BK all articles by the press concerning them, so that appropriate action could be taken by the BK. Although this activity in itself was not illegal, the Nazis hated and feared Father for doing this. So for that reason alone they tried to trip him up and wear him down with all these interrogations.

Also, during every Sunday service, Father read from the pulpit a list of names of those clergymen who were still in jail or had lately been arrested. This was, of course, forbidden, but he did it to save lives, because the Nazis hated any publicity about their persecutions. Soon, now, during every one of Father's services, two to three Gestapo agents

Father and his vicar, Pastor N (whose borrowed canoe Hans & I capsized) with a confirmation class of loyal parish girls. Herr Pastor N survived and became a bishop in Berlin.

sat in the church among the congregation, writing down everything Father read off his list. But every parishioner knew who they were, and no one sat near them, so they stuck out like sore thumbs. Father shook their hands at the door after services, just like he shook everyone else's, and wished them well. At least most of them blushed, and one even whispered to Father, "I am so sorry, but I must do my duty."

Besides these 60 interrogations, the following were listed for me by my parents after the war:

- Jailed in Moabit prison (Berlin) for two weeks.
- Jailed in Lehrter Street Prison (Berlin) several days.
- In "protective custody" in the cellar of Gestapo headquarters, Saarland Street (Berlin) for two days. (In this place, several BK clergy were beaten until they were crippled for life).
- Under house arrest (in our apartment) for two weeks.
- Arrested together with Dr. Martin Miermöller, Dr. Asmussen, Superintendent Jacobi, and several other leaders of the German BK, and held at the Alexander Platz prison for one day.
- Relieved of his duties as a pastor for several weeks.
- His salary stopped for an extended period of time.
- Incarcerated in the dreaded Columbia Haus (in Hasenheide, near Berlin), a concentration camp.

I knew at the time that he was in a concentration camp. Most Germans had never heard of these places, because even to mention them was punishable. But, of course, Jews, Gypsies, "enemies of the Reich" (which included BK Lutherans and resisting priests and nuns) and their families and friends knew what they were. So after 1945 I finally found out some details as to why he was taken there, and what happened.

A newsman from Reuter (the wire service of the British Press) showed up at our apartment one day and asked Father to meet with him and other foreign journalists secretly once a week to give them all the news about the latest arrests, people sent to jails, tortures (when known to the BK), murders or disappearances of BK pastors—complete with names, dates, and places. Father knew full well if he consented and the Nazis caught on to him he would be tortured and then executed. But he also knew that, if he took that chance, he would save many lives, because in those years the Nazis still wanted to be considered "civilized" by the rest of the world. Hitler would, if found out, have to stop or at least to curtail his henchmen. After consulting with Mother and his assistant he agreed.

He met secretly then once a week at a tiny, inconspicuous restaurant with Reuter and Basel and Stockholm correspondents. Now the London Times and the New York Times (through Reuter, also) and Basel and Stockholm printed the truth about BK persecutions by Hitler and his cohorts. The articles always quoted an "unknown" or an "anonymous source." Father did not even reveal to the BK itself that he was the source, in order not to endanger the entire Lutheran resistance movement. It was a highly dangerous and very lonely activity.

The Nazis were livid. They immediately suspected Father, because they knew he was press liaison for the BK with the German press. But they simply could not prove it, because as prearranged by Father and his assistant, whenever they arrested or interrogated Father, his assistant would meet in his stead with the foreign press and the articles would keep on appearing everywhere!

The BK was jubilant about the publicity about their plight. Soon the Nazis were forced to release many clergymen who were incarcerated, and a lot fewer were newly arrested.

But the Gestapo kept hounding Father. They bugged our apartment (through a wall in my parent's bedroom via the neighboring apartment house). Our phone was tapped, also. But we were wise to it and took many precautions. In frustration, the Gestapo then went directly to their leaders, and we found out eventually that Heydrich himself had given orders for Father to be interrogated once more, and, if that did not work, to take him to the Columbia Haus to be grilled further and to see if the news leak to the foreign press would then stop. (Heydrich, who was a stand-in for the infamous Himmler, was eventually assassinated in the Polish village of Lidice. The city was then totally flattened by the SS and all the townspeople were murdered.)

According to Mother's memoirs, two uniformed SS men came to our apartment and placed Father under arrest. While they waited for him to dress and get his ever-ready prison suitcase, Mother offered them coffee and eventually brought the conversation around to Father's arrest. In her journal she wrote:

> I said, "Tomorrow morning I will start to look for my husband."
> "That will be difficult, ma'am," one of them said, "because the order is coming from high up."
> "Oh, you mean from Hitler, Himmler, or Heydrich?"
> The man smiled and did not answer.

She knew then that the order had come directly from one of the three most dangerous men in all of Germany.

After a sleepless night she was awakened by a neighboring BK minister, Pastor Walter. Rumors had already reached him that Father had been arrested by the SS. He asked Mother if she knew where they had taken him, and when she said no he replied, "I hope not to the concentration camp at Hasenheide. I have just buried an inmate from there, a restaurateur, whom they had shot in the chest, directly through the Iron Cross First Class medal (the highest honor earned by soldiers of WW I)." He prayed with Mother and left. Shortly thereafter Father's assistant answered an anonymous phone call. "Frau Dr. Harnisch should come tomorrow at 5:00 PM to the Ministry of Internal Affairs, first floor, right hallway." Was this a trap? Would the Gestapo be waiting for her there? Would her children then have neither parent left? But she had to go, for she knew it might be her only chance to find out where Father had been taken.

She had hardly arrived at the appointed time in the designated hallway when a young man hurried past her and whispered, "Are you the wife of Dr. Harnisch?" Mother nodded. He whispered, "Your husband is in the Columbia Haus." She was unfamiliar with that name so she asked back, "The Columbia Haus?" He hurried past her once more and whispered, "Yes, the Columbia Haus!" And then he was gone.

Further inquiries from the BK then revealed to her that Columbia Haus was indeed the concentration camp in Hasenheide about which pastor Walter had warned her.

A few days later on a Sunday afternoon she took the train to the town of Hasenheide, located not too far from Berlin. After much asking around she was finally sent to an immense, forbidding building. Every window in it had closed shutters. In a small garden in front stood two guards who talked. Behind them she could see a huge gate with guardhouses. Mother wrote:

I walked up and down, despairing, praying, and trying to think. Suddenly I heard a man singing! I thought immediately that this could only be my joyful, God-trusting husband, who could sing in a place like this. I walked quickly by the two outside guards, greeting them cordially. They did not stop me and thought evidently that I had a visitor's permit. But at the gate, five young guys, ages about 18-20, ordered me sternly to halt. From their dialect they were Saxons, rather than Berlin natives. The Nazis used Saxons frequently as their henchmen, because Berliners were too good-natured.

"Do you have a permit to enter?"

"No."

"Then get out of here! Vamoose!"

"How do I get a permit? I see on this bulletin board that an inmate fell ill—that could be my husband, Dr. Harnisch!"

"No," they lied, "he is not here!"

"Wouldn't you be searching for family members if they had suddenly been arrested?"

There was no answer. I left for home feeling somewhat more comforted by the thought that at least I had found out where my husband was being held.

To find out how Father had fared after being arrested in our apartment, his memoirs mention that he was first taken to the local police station, questioned briefly and kept overnight in the busy station itself, on a cot rather than in a cell. Since sleep was impossible, a cop brought him wine to make him sleepy, but even after drinking half the bottle on an empty stomach, sleep would not come.

Next morning he was driven to the infamous seat of the Gestapo.

Soon I was introduced to assessor Chantré, a man known for his brutality. I will never forget this particular interrogation, because I was very aware that any rash answer could cost me my life. The assessor at once snapped at me nastily, "We know everything about you. You have supplied the foreign press with information about the church battle. There is no use denying this!" But I denied it nevertheless.

As the interrogation continued, Father decided that he should try to find out just how much the Gestapo did know.

I mentioned casually that a representative of Reuter had visited me. The assessor's face portrayed surprise and he said, "You are connected with him also?" I was sure now that I had won the game, because if he did not even know this then that meant that he knew absolutely nothing! I answered, "It's not my fault that the man visited me. That would only matter if I gave him any information, and I did not give him any."

After he spent another hour in vain to find out anything from me, he said somewhat more politely, "We'll have to find out now if your statements are correct. Until then we'll have to keep you here." I was escorted down several steps to the infamous Gestapo cellar. My cell was about one and a quarter meters wide and three meters long. The door was made of iron bars, through which a patrolling guard watched me constantly. Opposite, a small shaft let in some light, but there, too, I heard a guard patrolling. That meant I was watched from both sides. I spent the entire day sitting on a small stool. At night a cot was unfolded from the wall. This second night, too, I spent nearly sleepless, as the heavy steps of the guards woke me up continuously.

The next morning I was taken from the cell and spent hours in a large room, which filled up more and more with fellow sufferers. Between us sat heavily armed SS men, who made sure that no one exchanged a single word with anyone else. Toward noon, we were loaded into two "Green Minnas." We were pressed together like sardines, again watched by armed SS men. I was unable to tell where we were going. Finally we stopped. We were received by a horde of SS men who shouted foul-language epithets at us and drove us like cattle into a huge brick building.

Father at first shared a cell with a 16-year-old. He was a very dirty and very hungry youngster from an impoverished family who had tried to earn some money as a homosexual streetboy and was caught. Father found out from him that Columbia Haus was the first concentration camp ever built by the Nazis. And he also knew now that this place held only homosexuals (whom the Nazis hated and persecuted) and political prisoners.

Father decided to go on a hunger strike. He felt no hunger at first, anyway. And the food was so awful that he gladly gave the boy his share. He describes his meals as follows:

Breakfast was one slice of bread and a horrible yellowish fluid which was called coffee and served in a disgusting, peeling enamel cup. Dinner at noon was served in an equally disgusting bowl, and consisted of cabbage or barley broth with one potato in it. Supper was a repetition of breakfast. Meat was only served on Sundays, and it consisted of a piece of pig belly not bigger than a five-Mark coin.

My cellmate's happiness did not last long, though, because the commanding guard, a SS corporal, thought I would be better off with a different cellmate. This one was a Catholic attorney who had aided several struggling nuns' cloisters by smuggling in foreign currency for them. He had been a strong man, but was now so emaciated that his trousers could have accommodated a second person. Since suspenders were removed from everyone as they entered the concentration camp, his trousers would have dropped altogether had he not managed to get a hold of a piece of string. It was normally forbidden to own string, but he had become a trustee, and was permitted to scrub the halls daily. So the string held up his pants.

The rules of this KZ (German abbreviation for concentration camp) demanded that one was to jump up from one's stool if the door opened. Then one had to assume an erect military posture in the center of the cell, and one had to announce, "KZ inmate Harnisch, arrested because of connection to the foreign press." To the fury of all entrants, I changed the words as follows: "KZ inmate Harnisch, arrested because of being falsely accused of having connections to the foreign press." All their yelling at me did not stop me from repeating this over and over.

On my first few days there I had many opportunities to say my little verse. Because I was the first clergyman ever to be held there, I was exhibited like a monkey in a zoo. Every few minutes the door would open and my guard would show me to another SS man. These visits pretty much occurred in similar fashion. The visitor would ask me at first affably who I was. When I answered that I was a Protestant clergyman, he would laugh loudly and sarcastically. "Oh, you are a preacher pig? In that case you got lots of time here for praying." After other spiteful remarks, the door was slammed shut until it opened again and I was again stared at like a rare species. Finally, the last one of the SS company had inspected me. Since my cellmate, understandably, spent as much time as possible dawdling with his mop in the hallways, I had now much time to think.

Father described his thoughts during the first few days there. He mainly agonized about two things. One was the fact that he had lied (about his connection to the foreign press) in order to save his life. To him, any lie was a terrible sin against God, which weighed heavily on him now. But he finally convinced himself that the Bible only forbids lying to one's friends, and the Nazis were his enemy. And if this still was a sin, then God would hopefully forgive him.

His second thought was his hunger strike. He had announced it, and was then permitted one hour after meals to take the food to the toilet off the hall, which prisoners were permitted to use once an hour. But he was not permitted to give the food to a cellmate. This now, as well as thinking of his wife and children in case of his death, made him change his mind about the hunger strike. He decided to gag down the food, and he even managed to say grace.

He had tried not to think much about us at home during the first two days, but on the third day a deep depression overcame him, as was rather typical for all prisoners. The thought that he would never see us again overwhelmed him, and he broke down and started to cry. But the thought of the ever-watching SS (through a peephole in the door) enjoying his breakdown made him decide to praise God instead of making Satan happy.

The hymn Praise be to the Lord *seemed the most appropriate in this situation. My further thought was, if I am going to sing I might as well sing on the top of my voice to comfort as many fellow inmates as possible. With that I positioned myself in the middle of the cell and roared, rather than sang, "Praise be to the Lord, the mighty King of all Honor." I had just started the second verse when the door was flung open. "Shut your trap, you goddamned preacher pig. You are not in the movies!" But the first verse alone had already worked a true miracle.*

This, of course, referred to Mother's recognizing his voice as she walked up and down despairingly in front of the building, trying to figure out if he was really in there.

At this point we return to Mother's memoirs. She now made an appointment with a director of the Ministry of the Interior in order to get the permit needed to visit Father in the Columbia Haus. His name was Dr. Buttman, and she had heard through the BK that this man had sympathy for persecuted BK members. He had even managed once to prevent Pastor Rahmel's incarceration in a concentration camp.

At the appointed time she found herself in the Ministry, in the oversized study of Dr. Buttman. She wrote:

After I had stated my case and asked for the permit, Dr. Buttman said, "I must ask you one question!"

"Please do, Herr Director of the Ministry."

"Did your husband—on his own—have dealings with the world press?"

I blushed deeply and paused. I was thinking that his study was probably bugged, too. I smiled and answered with a drawn out no. He smiled back. He had understood. He gave me the permit.

The rowdies at the Columbia Haus stared in disbelief as I reappeared not only once, but twice with a permit to visit my husband.

The commander of this concentration camp was absolutely amazed and curious how I had gotten, by luck or nerve, a very rare visitor's permit. He personally led me through six ceiling-high gates to my husband's cell. My husband was speechless when he saw me, and then he was overjoyed. He said, "I will never forget that you found me, and that you had the courage to come here!" Finally I asked him, "What things do you need most?" He mentioned a few items. Later in life, my husband often burst out laughing how I had ordered the commandant to write everything down since I had no paper and pencil with me. And he obeyed. At my next visit I brought him the things he had asked for, such as soap and a hand towel, handkerchiefs, and such.

Father's memoirs described his amazement and jubilance when she showed up in his cell. She and other BK members had also pressured the Gestapo by phone to grant him medical supervision. He now was seen by a doctor every other day—although in a grimy sickbay—for his heart problems, his emaciation, and his terribly inflamed hip (from sleeping on a wood pallet). This also helped to relieve the awful monotony of sitting day after day in his cell without permission to read or write anything. To quote Father:

A less pleasant diversion was the daily roll call in the hall, where we stood in erect military position sometimes hours on end, about one meter from each other. This gave the guards a welcome opportunity to deride and to torture us. I remember how my neighbor was grabbed by his hair, and his head was slammed against the wall over and over again. I was so aware it was only my lie that kept me from the horror cell downstairs in the cellar of this place!

Once, by chance, I was placed next to a newly arrived inmate, who was a Catholic priest. When I tried to whisper to him, the SS guard yelled, "Who talked?" When I kept silent he flew into a rage. But my cellmate, who had been slowly scrubbing the floor, came to my rescue. He said, "I had asked the gentleman to move a little, since I had to scrub beneath his feet." This made sense to the guard and I was saved once again.

Despite the order of silence, amazingly a whisper campaign worked well. I now knew who was behind various cell doors, and why they had been arrested. One was a (military) captain who had earned many medals in WWI, but who had somehow aroused Hitler's wrath. Another was a prominent leader in the Hitler youth, but he had done something unconventional. He now tried hard to escape from his miserable situation here by exhibiting an exaggerated "correct military" posture at all times and by being a "model prisoner." And there was a tiny Jewish man, who had gotten drunk once and bragged about his hoarding of foreign currency. Several of the homosexual prisoners belonged in a mental institution. One, for instance, a 16-year-old, was also a masochist, who felt mainly aroused if tortured. He fell in love with our most brutal SS guard. While on duty in the SS dining room, he purposely smashed a china plate directly at the feet of his idol. He then stood entranced as the vicious man vented his rage on him. These things I found out immediately through the successful whisper campaign.

Probably the worst experience was the night preceding a transfer of many inmates to a different KZ, farther away from Berlin, in order to make room for new arrivals. The transport was to take place at 9:00 AM the next morning. To prepare these unfortunates for their next existence in other KZs, they were tortured here yet. At midnight I heard thunderous rapping on several cell doors. Ten minutes later the victims were lined up in the hall and then "exercised"—they were chased all night long to run through the halls around us. When they collapsed from exhaustion, we heard them screaming as they were kicked up by heavy boots and beaten until they continued running. I was only able to sleep a few minutes at a time until this pitiful column was chased by my door again. I thought of the horror I had experienced *in a slaughterhouse yard once, when the exhausted animals were beaten brutally as they raced to their death. This went on until 7:00 AM when the men stood sweat-soaked in the ice-cold court-yard until they were finally loaded into vans.*

I could talk here about many further tortures, but this is probably enough.

Father described his days as creeping by slowly "amid fear and shock." But there was one welcome exception, namely the first day of May, which was "Labor Celebration Day." This was the most fanatically observed holiday by thousands of flag-swinging, marching, military-song-singing Nazis in parades. Most of Father's SS guards were celebrating, while all the inmates were locked into their cells. Even Father's cellmate did not spend the day scrubbing. He and Father made chess figures out of torn bits of paper, and played chess all day on an improvised board. He saved those paper bits as souvenirs. He could also finally lie on his pallet during the day, and he kept looking up to that small barred window in the ceiling, enjoying hugely the pouring rain coming down on all those Nazi parades.

Mother was still trying to figure out how she could get Father out.

How could I get my husband out of the concentration camp? I finally decided to go to the highest instance, namely, Secretary of the Interior Frick. I went to the Ministry of the Interior and was stopped almost immediately at the portal by two uniformed soldiers.

"Do you have an audience permit?"
"No."

They took me to an anteroom and had me fill out an application, to which I added: "This is a matter of life or death for a human being."

The soldier looked sad when he brought the application back to me. "No, his Excellency the Minister of the Interior regrets."

What now? I'm standing in the anteroom, totally at a loss. I simply cannot get myself to leave. Suddenly the door opens, and two gentlemen enter. One of them is robed in the Lutheran clergy frock with a large golden cross on his chest, the other a younger gentleman. The latter introduces himself to me. I recognize the name. So this is Count T. The other one has to be Hitler's Reichbishop himself. I approach him politely. "Your Honor the Reichbishop."

"Yes."

"I am the wife of Pastor Harnisch. I beg you to have my husband released from the concentration camp Columbia Haus."

Count T answers instead, "He is not being treated badly."

Now I answer firmly and forcefully, "I have seen him. There is hardly any daylight in his cell—only a tiny, barred window in the ceiling. Despite his ailing hip he has to sleep on wooden planks. Not even a hand towel. An SS man had said to him, 'Dry your hands on a shirt, preacher pig!' Every half hour the SS man and his comrades haul him out of his cell and swear and laugh at him and show him around to other SS men like a wild animal in a zoo."

Count T repeats, "I cannot believe he is being treated there that badly."

I ask, "Your Excellency the Count. Have you ever been in a concentration camp? Besides, my business is with his Excellency the Reichbishop here."

Reichbishop Müller now, somewhat intimidated, starts: "I did not give the order to have your husband arrested. There is nothing I can do. I only see them (Hitler, Himmler, and Heydrich) rarely."

Now I answer forcefully, "Since YOU are in charge of all church matters, I demand that YOU get my husband released by this coming Sunday, so he can preach his sermon. You should consider how much you are hurting your own cause by keeping a clergyman incarcerated who is so well-known and loved!"

The Reichbiship repeated once more, subdued, "I cannot do anything in this affair."

I answered firmly, "YOUR CHURCH (the DC) has put my husband into the concentration camp. It is now up to YOU to get him out. And remember that he has to preach Sunday!" I then nodded and left.

Like a wildfire, news of his arrest had spread through all of Berlin. Already at the subway station a group of parishioners was patiently awaiting my return to hear if I had managed to free my husband.

After Father's imprisonments, grateful, brave and poor parishioners sent flowers every October 9th on his birthday.

The next morning the phone rang. "Here T, His Excellency the Reichbishop, is informing you that this afternoon at 3:00 PM your husband will be released from the Columbia Haus. His Excellency the Reichbishop would be pleased if you would thank him personally." I answered, "Your Excellency the Count, the church of your Reichbishop has incarcerated my husband, so it was up to the Reichbishop to get him out. I will not come, but I thank you for your notification." I hung up, period.

And at 4:00 PM that day (Saturday, one day before his sermon) my husband was home again.

Coming Up for Air

1935 to 1937

As I mentioned once before, in the fall of 1935 I enrolled in a private lyzeum for girls. In Germany, the great majority of children stay in the basic, elementary schools and graduate from those at about age 16. Then they usually attend a trade school or go to work in factories or shops. The higher educational institutions are called lyzeums for girls, and *gymnasiums* for boys. They are prep schools for universities, though not all students choose to finish, or to take the final exam, the dreaded *Abitur*, at about age 17.

Lyzeums and gymnasiums simply want only the children of the rich, namely those who can afford the stiff tuition, for which there is no state aid available. These kids, of course, also have to have the brains to pass a tough entrance exam. Odi had mastered hers two years earlier, and somehow I managed to pass, also. Of course, our parents could not afford to pay the tuition for one, much less for two girls. But this particular lyzeum was a private school. It was owned and operated by a grand lady, Dr. Christ, a member of the BK who waived tuition for both Odi and me. That is not to say that she was anymore lenient with us than with anyone else. She ran the school with iron discipline, yet she was always fair in all her decisions.

It took me an hour and ten minutes to walk to school now. My parents gave me a dime to spend per school day. This coin offered me one of three possibilities: a subway ride partway to school, a subway ride partway from school, or one ice cream cone from a parlor next to school. You guessed it—I usually chose the cone. Especially because the ice cream parlor was the favorite after-school hangout for many of the students, and for some good-looking boys from the nearby gymnasium.

My lyzeum had originally been two adjoining apartment houses. But now only the front had apartments, which were used by Dr. Christ and her teachers. The rear apartments had been converted into classrooms, an auditorium, and a gym. There was no cafeteria in any German school, but Mother had more knowledge about nutrition than most parents in those days; she added fruits and nuts to our sandwich. In the winter the fruit was dried.

Our curriculum was immediately very stiff: French, chemistry, algebra, biology, geography, history, German essay writing, music, sports, and art. Most of these subjects were taught daily, so we carried a heavy load of textbooks back and forth to school daily. In later years, English, physics, and geometry were added. And school lasted eight to nine hours daily, including Saturdays.

It did not take me long to decide which teachers I "hated," which I "adored" (few), and a few in-betweens. Most were spinsters and not a male teacher in sight. Soon my excitement about learning French now subsided. Not only did the innumerable irregular verbs drive me up the wall, but the teacher, too. She was white-haired, black-dressed, gaunt and nasty, and she obviously enjoyed terrorizing generations of children.

But still, it was fun to show off with my French in my neighborhood, where no one ever went to a lyzeum. Then a classmate and I decided it would be even more fun to impress subway riders. She had, of course, more money than I did and she paid for the trip. We took the subway toward the west of Berlin and conversed loudly in our lousy French. Then one of the riders got up—a good-looking young man. He approached and addressed us in a flow of rapid, perfect French, also quite loudly. We blushed and stood silent, neither understanding one word nor being able to say anything. Then—as he got ready to get off the train—he smiled and said, "Au revoir, my little Berlin-Parisiennes." And several people around us laughed and laughed. I was cured once and for all from ever showing off again with my so-called "higher education."

We had spent a terrifying winter and spring with Father having been interrogated by the Gestapo downtown countless times. Each time we did not know if he would be returned to us, and he always had his prison suitcase packed, just in case.

Because church and state were not separated and clergymen were paid from taxes for an entire year, Father's salary was now suddenly stopped, too. The BK chipped in, and our parishioners collected at the church door for us at every service.

The three of us at a parish outing, 1937

An amazing thing happened to us then as the summer vacation started. The Nazis had already tightened the German borders against many travelers, especially the Jews. And Switzerland was not particularly known as a welcoming host for political dissenters and refugees. But for that summer of 1936 many Swiss families decided to give us German children of persecuted churchmen a much-needed six-weeks break from stress. About 200 children—whose fathers had been or still were imprisoned— were invited to spend the summer vacation in Switzerland. And amazingly the Nazis allowed us to cross the border.

So the three of us traveled with other Berlin children to Munich, where BK clergymen's children from all over Germany assembled and were then taken by a special train to Lake Constance. A Swiss ferry awaited us and we all sang happily as we crossed this huge lake 'til we arrived at the Swiss shore.

Stress relief started immediately: No one gave the Nazi salute of "Heil Hitler," no one wore those brown uniforms, and no one ordered us around in military fashion. And we were even asked which siblings wanted to stay together. Odi chose to be by herself, and a nice family in the nearby old town of Trogen was her host for the six weeks.

Hans and I wanted to stay together, so at least for three weeks a physician couple was able to take both of us. They were wealthy and childless and lived in a suburb of nearby

St. Gallen. I remember mainly learning and then playing the game of croquet, which had been unknown in Germany. With our usual passion, Hans and I played many hours on our host's lawn every day, with their little Dachshund running around us excitedly and trying in vain to retrieve stray balls from the bushes, which were much too heavy for it. We even sneaked out of the house on moonlit nights to continue our game on the silvery, dewy lawn.

After the three weeks were up, our hosts went on their own vacation, so they paid for a summer camp in nearby Gais for me, and paid the train fare for Hans to the high alpine part of Switzerland where he stayed with a clergy couple near the gorgeous *Jungfrau* Alp. All that scenery was totally wasted on Hans there, as he had never been away from any of us for three weeks, and some very picturesque but tear-smudged cards arrived from him in Berlin.

I loved every minute in that summer camp. There were no bullies at all among the kids, and the counselors (all female) were kind and spoiled us. The food was delicious, especially after Mother's horrendous cooking. Like Heidi I thrived on milk and cheese and crisp, round bread. And I felt even more like Heidi when we were taken on mountain hikes and came across tiny mountain farms with deep slanting roofs and peaceful, climbing goats.

Once I led a group of smaller girls to a nearby pasture to find wildflowers. We climbed over the wood-rail fence, paying little attention to a herd of cows grazing farther up on the mountain. Suddenly I heard the bell of the lead cow coming rapidly closer. She was tearing down the mountain toward us. I yelled and we raced to the fence and clambered over it moments before the furious cow—head down—rammed her horns into the fence. Two of us girls had worn red outfits, and Swiss cows are very aware that they all have very dangerous horns.

There was a mid-sized mountain between Trogen where Odi was, and Gais, where I was. Odi wrote me a card and suggested a date and time when we should meet on top of the mountain. The camp ladies fixed me some great provisions and lots of water for the hot climb. I started out early in the morning, making sure I had nothing red on me. After about six hours of climbing I reached the top, where Odi was already waiting for me and sketching the fabulous view. We exchanged all our experiences and our food; we sang and picked wildflowers. We were just high up enough to find the lovely blue, crocus-like gentian, and the wood-stemmed, bright red Alpine rose, but not high enough for edelweiss. And we both were back in our respective valleys before dark.

Swiss schools start somewhat earlier with classes after summer vacations than do German schools. I was allowed to stay on yet for another week after most of the kids had left camp already. I was even permitted to attend any class I wanted at the Swiss school, where I told them some of the horrors of the Third Reich. Several moved teachers asked me why we were not fleeing the country. I told them Father had had several offers from England and other countries including Switzerland, but decided to stay because he did not want to desert his suffering BK parish. Best of all I liked the Swiss music class, where the teacher and children taught me about ten Swiss anthems and folk songs, some of those in a thick, Swiss-German dialect. And I even learned how to yodel!

When I got back to Berlin, I—for once—looked forward to school starting so I could brag about my heavenly Swiss vacation. And then I taught my classmates and my music teacher all those Swiss freedom songs. And some even learned how to yodel from me.

Berlin's beautiful zoo, aquarium, and numerous museums were a source of great enjoyment to us children. At first accompanied by Odi, who usually sketched while we investigated, Hans and I were finally allowed to occasionally visit these places on our own, usually on Sundays after church. Even our sparse family budget did not prevent our parents from making these educational trips possible for us.

Movies were forbidden, though, despite my going on 12 now. Hans and I envied all our friends and classmates who long had seen movies and talked about them so much. Hans yearned to see Tarzan and I was enraged that I was not allowed to see Shirley Temple tap dance. So one spring Sunday afternoon, Hans and I supposedly took the subway to a museum, but instead we got off two stations sooner at the Alexander Circle. In those days that was a miniature Times Square, with many cheap little movie houses. So now our museum money permitted me to see the adored Shirley, while Hans admired his hero Tarzan next door. It was getting dark when we met outside, and we hurried home. Father asked casually what we had seen at the museum today. We lied brilliantly but in vain—Father had called the museum and found out that it had closed at four o'clock already. If we had not lied we would not have been punished too harshly, but in our house lying was a capital sin, so we got punished severely. Yet, when in later years we saw movies, nothing ever came close again to the happiness we had experienced when we first saw Tarzan and Shirley.

Uncle Siegfried, Father's older, stern brother, was a career officer in the German army's corps of engineers. He had risen very high in rank. We overheard Father arguing with him in his study. Father felt that one should not serve in the army as long as Hitler ran the country, while Uncle Siegfried felt that the army "had nothing to do with politics." During these visits, Hans and I were stuck with entertaining our smaller cousins Wilhelm and Joachim in our playroom. We cared little for their company, especially since they enjoyed making us mad by urinating into the humidifier, which was hanging from our playroom radiator.

We did like Uncle Alexander, Father's adopted younger brother, very much. He had a soft beard and was warm and kind. He was also one of my godfathers, and on every baptismal anniversary he gave or sent me a present, such as a large amber pendant exquisitely mounted, or an amber necklace. He also started an entire silver cutlery set for me, to which he added many pieces in my lifetime. Uncle Alex was a brilliant engineer for the Siemens Works, and he was highly paid. We all kept it a family secret that Uncle Alex was Jewish, because the anti-Semitic hate propaganda had been started by Hitler long before he even took power. And now we really started to fear for his life, and that of his wife and two sons, who were Odi's and my age, because more and more Jews in our neighborhood were disappearing.

Odi and I were invited to Uncle Alexander's villa when I was 12 and Odi was 14. It was located so far outside of Berlin that one had to take a regular train to get there. At arrival we were picked up with their chauffeured limousine. We lived in luxury for that week, and our cousins Ulf and Gero entertained us with things like billiards and target shooting. There was even a Newfoundland dog, and a marble goldfish pond in the garden, complete with fountain. Aunt Gertrud had a macaw parrot perching next to her in a ring on a stand, where she cooed to it and fed it goodies. We were afraid of her. She was silent much of the time, but watched everyone closely while lounging on a couch in exotic robes, a long silver cigarette holder in her mouth. Her family and the maids and the cook all seemed to be intimidated by her. She preferred me quite obviously to Odi, but even when she fed me expensive chocolates I felt uncomfortable. Odi and I had also noted with disgust that a Nazi flag flew from a pole in front of the villa.

Only when we were adults did my parents disclose to us the horrible truth about Aunt Gertrud. She was a fanatic Nazi and drove her husband nearly to insanity by constantly threatening him to disclose to the Nazis that he was a Jew. He was practically her prisoner during Hitler's reign. They had an apartment in the city, also, to which she invited me time and again. My parents did not dare to arouse her ire, either, because of her Nazi threats, and I was asked repeatedly to visit her. Eventually we all realized that she was planning to marry me to her son Gero. When Gero and I caught on to this, we discussed it first with each other and then confronted her together and informed her that we had no intentions whatsoever to marry, even in the future. She finally stopped inviting me then, but Uncle Alexander's living hell with her continued. Ironically, she died of cancer at the end of the war, when Uncle Alexander could have divorced her safely.

Occasionally we were allowed to keep a pet, mainly a frog or a goldfish. But there were also three exciting ones. The first one was an exotic land turtle, about the size of a dinner plate. It had beautiful orange markings and ate everything from our fingers. We fashioned a harness for it to which we snapped a leash, and then we took it for outings on the sidewalk. The neighbor kids loved it, but adults always thought it should be in water. The first winter we let it hibernate in the cool cellar, but in the second winter we were too lazy to take it there, and just let it sleep under the playroom couch. Mother had daily help from developmentally challenged or epileptic girls from a neighborhood shelter, who were fed and paid and treated kindly by us. They probably did not know about the turtle, and swished it against the wall daily with their wet mops, while we were in school. We felt very guilty and sad when the poor turtle did not wake up in the spring.

Another memorable pet was a mourning dove. It also became incredibly tame. I remember this gentle bird walking around on the dinner table while we ate, daintily nibbling on items off our plates and then leaving green spinach footprints all over the white tablecloth. Its wings were slightly trimmed and we always left the balcony door wide open when the weather allowed. But one sunny day, while perching on the balcony box, the bird lost its balance and half fell, half flew down unto the awning of a barbershop close by. Before we could get downstairs to retrieve our dove, a passerby threw his hat over it and then used his cane to bring it down to him. By the time we got to the street he had disappeared with our bird.

The third pet was a little black and white, longhaired dog. It was a stray and had followed Mother home. She did not have the heart to leave it out in the sleet and cold. Hans and I were jubilant, but this little dog had many bad manners, and since we were in school much of the day, Mother was stuck with it. At night we kept the dog in Hans's half-bath to keep it out of trouble.

One night one of Father's assistants was working late. We were all sleeping and he headed for that toilet. Out jumped the little dog, scaring the heck out of him. The dog then ran all over the place, ending up in our playroom. In despair the man opened the balcony doors, and when the dog zoomed out he quickly shut the doors after it. Then he went home. We awoke to utter disaster. I had mentioned earlier that Mother stored all the food that spoiled on the balcony in the winter, and our little dog had raised absolute Cain. He had strewn the entire balcony with meats, vegetables, fish, butter and the like, all of it having been partly eaten, chewed on or played with. When we came home from school that day our pet was gone, and all our begging did not move Mother to reveal to us where she had taken that little dog. I guess it all goes to show that pets don't do too well in the city.

During that winter of '37, most of my classmates were taking ice-skating lessons. I walked for an hour every other day or so, even in the iciest of winter weather, to reach a skating rink. For several years I only had skates that screwed onto your shoes and would often come off suddenly, causing you to take bad spills. All my classmates, of course, had figure skates and short twirly skirts. I felt clumsy and humiliated, especially when I watched the others getting expensive skating lessons from a handsome male teacher, whom females of every age simply adored. Even worse was the fact that I had no money to spend on a delicious, non-alcoholic hot toddy, which was sold in the "warming-up room" next to the rink. That's where everyone congregated. When at age 14 my parents finally gave me a pair of figure skates for Christmas, which were brown instead of white, I had pretty much outgrown my love for skating by then, anyway.

To be a poor clergyman's daughter in a class full of rich girls was hard on my ego. I knew, of course, that my whole family was suffering because of our martyrdom, but

I still hated my sister's hand-me-downs, which had not even been fashionable in the first place. The sweaters bothered me the most, since they had shrunk considerably over the years while I was now maturing considerably.

It didn't help, either, that some of the girls in my class were one, two, or even three years older than I. They had to repeat school years because they were not very bright. Chances are that they never passed the lyzeum's entrance exam in the first place, but had been accepted because the school was struggling financially. They had long been wearing make-up and high heels and had good-looking young men waiting for them at the ice cream parlor after school. Although I did not always envy them, I helped them often with undone homework and noticed with embarrassment that the teachers totally ignored them or called them "hopeless stupids." Nevertheless, I adored especially Ursula, a wealthy physician's daughter who had scores of boys and men vying for her attention. I was terribly flattered that she actually liked me, for these older girls simply could not be bothered with us "kids." She even bought me an occasional ice cream cone, or introduced me to one of her male fans. One day after gym, as she let me help her brush her gorgeous hair, she said, "Gisela, I know you don't think of yourself as pretty. But believe me, you have good facial structure. Don't worry, when you get older you will be very pretty." I laughed bitterly and said, "Yea, as pretty as you." But she said seriously, "No, prettier." She was probably exaggerating, but my heart jumped with joy. She saved me years of agony and complexes. I stopped despairing about my looks from that moment on.

Hans was now nine, and my parents had enrolled him in the famous gymnasium called the *Graue Kloster*, or "Grey Cloister." And grey it was, an absolute horror for Hans.

Father was determined to give Hans the very best "humanistic" education, hopefully leading to the study of theology. My poor brother, who had absolutely no intention of becoming a clergyman, was now forced to learn Latin, Greek, and eventually even Hebrew, besides all other difficult academic subjects. He loathed the "Grey Cloister" and everything it offered. My parents spent countless hours to help a grim and often tearful Hans with his homework and punished him when he "did not apply himself."

There were days when Hans and I talked about running away, and one Sunday after church we actually attempted it. We packed plenty of provisions, informed everyone we were going for a daytrip, and then we took off with our bikes. We rode all the way out eastward until we arrived at our beloved cove. It was fall and the boat was long back in its homeport. Since we were now "free and on our own" we decided to investigate the big sandpit in the middle of the pine forest. It was being mined on weekdays and had been strictly "off limits" to us children. There were lorries on rails on top, and we decided to try a ride. We climbed into the first lorry and loosened the brake, and away we went. But halfway down the mountain it picked up incredible speed and started to tip at a curve. Hans and I jumped simultaneously and went head over heels down the sand mountain. We did not break anything, but we were badly bruised and scraped. While we crawled painfully back up we decided that we would be best off heading home now—especially since it was getting dark already and the forest began to look eerie. Our parents happened to come home late that evening, also, so luckily no one was ever the wiser.

Father insisted that I attend two years of his confirmation class, instead of one year like everyone else. He also made me teach Sunday school from age 11 on. And I played flute in the parish youth orchestra, sang duets with Odi at every church bazaar in East Berlin, sang in the church choir, attended weekly parish youth group meetings, and on and on. Frankly, I was getting fed up with these overdoses of religious "musts."

The worst of it was that we pastor's children were watched closely from many windows by parish eyes, which had little else to look at in this quiet, drab neighborhood. If we used a swear word or behaved "undecorously" we were quickly reported to our parents, or much gossiped about. I resented bitterly to be permanently living in a glass house.

Once when I was about 12, Hans, Berthold and I were having a lusty snowball battle in a neighboring street. Some older boys appeared and joined in the fray, but I noticed Hans and Berthold wincing when they got hit, and saw the stones falling out of the snowballs. I raced toward that group and yelled at Hans and Berthold to run. They did, and I lit into the gang, livid with rage. Luckily some adult passersby rescued me soon, and I tore home to beat the gossips. Sure enough, I had barely finished telling my parents what had happened when the phone rang and some elderly ladies "just wanted to inform my parents that Gisela had been involved in a public brawl."

Despite all these eyes—or maybe because of them— Odi and I managed to start smoking secretly, and Odi used make-up when she was out somewhere, though she wiped every bit off before she got back to our neighborhood. We felt almost challenged to be a little bit bad. I lied more than Odi did, but I always felt that she was not nearly as harshly punished as I was. And whenever Mother spanked Hans I tried to interfere, and got spanked then, also. My sweet but dominated grandmother tried often in vain to rescue me.

Father never interfered. In his opinion, Mother was always right. Yet he himself suffered her fury. I knew, because I could hear her angry whispering late into the nights from their bedroom next to mine.

About two weeks before the summer vacation of 1937 I got hurt. Our gym teacher decided to make us use a "medicine ball"—as these huge, heavy balls were called—instead of a regular volleyball during a game in the lyzeum yard. These balls were occasionally used to increase muscle strength. I loved sports, and, as usual, was allowed to pick my own team. I heaved the ball with all my might, lost my balance and landed on my left elbow. It did not swell too badly, and our family doctor decided not to X-ray. He put the arm in a sling at an angle and prescribed aspirin. But the pain got more excruciating by the day, and after 13 days the doctor finally decided it should be X-rayed. I walked two miles to the nearest X-ray clinic and a technician looked at me rather seriously as she gave me the X-ray. Sure enough, the entire tip of my left elbow was nearly broken off, and the same doctor now straightened the arm and put it into a plaster cast. I was in agony and had a fever to boot.

The worst thing was that all arrangements had been made for our vacation, and I found myself on a train with Odi the very next day after my arm had been forced into the straight cast. It was the worst, all-night train ride in my life, and I did not give Odi a chance to sleep, either.

Hans would spend the summer in Beyersdorf at Aunt Oda's. But Odi and I would be in a south German village, and then in a Rhineland town toward the end of the vacation. Two clergymen had invited us for the summer. We did not know them personally, but they were BK members and wanted to give us some relief from Berlin.

I had even brought my bicycle along, and Odi and I now changed trains in Stuttgart and took a local train to Kirchheim. There we were supposed to be picked up at the station. We got my bike off the luggage car and looked around, but saw no one who resembled a clergyman. As the platform emptied we decided that the lone male figure there had to be our host. As he approached we almost decided to deny who we were. But that would have been a little difficult, for he had been given a description of us. One could not decide whether he was comical, or scary, or both. He was tiny and gaunt and his face was wrinkled, his nose huge, his eyes just slits, his black suit much too big for him, and—to top it all off—a big white, flat straw hat, the kind that had been popular before WWI. His thin smile and his high, crackly voice did not make us feel any better, either. Silently we loaded the bike into the trunk of his ancient car and just as silently we all sat stiffly as he drove about 10 mph, slightly zigzagging through the pretty, pre-alpine countryside to the little village Nabern.

But to our great surprise it turned out to be a wonderful vacation. The pastor disappeared immediately into his study from where he only appeared to eat, sleep or preach. He was single, a poet and philosopher, and totally misplaced in his role as a clergyman. The village totally ignored him, too. But he was BK and his heart must have been in the right place or he would not have invited us.

A live-in housekeeper—a middle-aged, gentle soul—fixed us wonderful meals, even *spätzle* with sauerbraten. She, too, left us totally to our own devices. We were only expected to make our own beds and appear at mealtimes.

The small parsonage nestled close to a 400-year-old simple stone church. A little garden connected the two buildings. It was the loveliest garden I had ever seen, blooming with every conceivable flower in sort of an ordered disorder. From a small vine-covered gazebo hung actual table grapes, which were not quite ripe yet. We could sit in there and write or paint, or just daydream. We filled our lungs with fresh, sweet scents, and soaked in the glorious display of brilliant colors and shapes. They varied from the tiniest purple violets to the tallest red mallows and golden sunflowers. The hedge consisted of raspberry, blackberry and elderberry bushes, and the only noise heard was the humming of busy bees. Even the windows from our bedroom granted us the view of the garden and the picturesque old church.

Odi spent most of the three weeks right there, painting and writing poetry. But I had much more interesting things to do. At least by now my fever had broken, and I tried to ignore the bad pain in my elbow. So with my heavy, useless plaster arm dangling by my side, I nevertheless managed to steer and ride my bike everywhere. Soon I made friends with some village girls, and they let me play with their pets and help milk their cows and brush their horses. Their parents took me with them to the fields in their empty wagons to return with hay, and I helped as best I could with my good arm. I was often invited for supper with home-baked dark breads and slabs of salted hams and various cheeses. And there was always cider and milk on the table. The flies were bad, though, and the stench terrible from the manure pits located often directly under the windows, because the living quarters of these small farms were located above the stables. When I first arrived I mistook a pump from one of those pits for a fresh-water pump, and a gush of liquid manure landed on me, just missing my open mouth. There was much village laughter about this little city slicker.

One day arrived Hansjörg, the 20-year-old nephew of our host. He was a BK clergyman's son from Stuttgart and an engineering student who loved spelunking. He also had his bike with him and took me along on his cave excursions. We rode to the beginning of the nearest mountain, and then climbed and searched by the hour 'til we found a sandstone cave. It was tough crawling through narrow openings with my inflexible arm, but Hansjörg helped me. We crawled around on our bellies with flashlights, looking for a tunnel to lead us farther into the mountain. It was usually in vain, but exciting anyway. Hansjörg knew much about fossil rocks, for which we searched. They featured sometimes very clear imprints of petrified sea animals from millions of years ago when all of this had been an ocean. There was a museum in a small town nearby, which had hundreds of wonderful fossils found in these mountains. Hansjörg and I also rode our bikes to Kirchheim and swam in the huge town pool there, with me holding my plaster cast way up into the air to keep it from getting wet. I was very grateful to Hansjörg, but Odi and I found him personally too pedantic and unattractive for our taste.

The three weeks seemed to fly, and we headed now by train for the Rhineland. A warm, childless clergy couple picked us up from the station and drove us to their home in a suburb. It was modern and bright, and it featured a great lawn with a friendly Newfoundland dog. There were thousands of fireflies floating above that lawn every night, and I caught them by the handful and planted them into the dog's long black coat until he glowed all over. The lawn had a sprinkler system and a long water hose, with which Odi and I cooled each other off during the very hot days there. I wore a bathing suit all day long, and paid little attention to the Rhine valley sun, which reddened my back and shoulders right along with the grapes, which were now ripening everywhere. Two days before our train trip home I had added a horrendous sunburn to my still sensitive arm, and was unable to get near the soft upholstery with my back as the train bumped and jolted me northward. Oh well—at least I had a grand vacation to remember.

Monsters Feel Invincible

1937 to 1940

B efore school started that fall, Mother finally conceded that I needed a few outfits of my own. The reason being that Odi had stopped growing, and I had suddenly shot up to her height in that single summer of the broken arm.

My self-esteem now rose with the inches I had so suddenly attained, and with every new dress, skirt, blouse, sweater or coat. Our poor parish seamstress was not too bright, but reasonable, and the clothes were at least passable. I was still forced to wear "clodhopper" shoes, though, and heavy socks, while my classmates long wore nylons and elegant shoes. But I had learned to soften my look by twisting my hair along the temples into rolls, and by doubling the hated pigtails upward toward my ears. And very gradually—in order not to arouse parental attention—I shaved the gap between my eyebrows, and even the eyebrows themselves a little.

Boys had not been much on my mind yet, but suddenly that winter, during one of the weekly parish youth group meetings, I felt the eyes of a boy on me. Whenever I looked back at him, he blushed and looked away. His name was Eberhard. He was tall and lanky, with almost white-blond hair and blue eyes. I wondered why I had never really noticed him before. I knew that his mother was a widow and that he was an only child. She always brought him to all parish functions, though they had a long walk to get to our church. She was a loyal, anti-Nazi BK member, and quite educated.

Eberhard told me now that he attended the very gymnasium close to my lyzeum! He was two grades above me and also an average student. I had the feeling he was quite lonely. I was proud that this shy and good-looking boy, who had evidently never dated anyone before, was interested in me. Odi had long started to date off and on, and I was not about to tell her about my growing interest in Eberhard. Nor did I enlighten anyone else, not even Hans.

To tell the truth, I was not head over heels in love. But it was exciting and flattering to be enviously watched by some of my classmates as I was escorted from the ice cream parlor by Eberhard. He carried my heavy briefcase as he accompanied me now daily to the outskirts of my neighborhood, from where we walked apart in order not to be seen as a "twosome" by the ever-vigilant parish eyes.

Several months passed before we finally dared to touch hands. And then, one spring day as I was nearing 13 and he 15, we decided to meet some evening in a park, two "el" stations away. It was very difficult for me to set a day and time, but I finally managed it. I faked a fitting with our seamstress at her apartment, and added a few other fictitious errands after supper. It was a bright, moonlit evening. I caught the "el" to the park, where Eberhard was waiting for me at the entrance. The place was nearly deserted, so we self-consciously linked arms and headed for one of the benches. I tried to lean close to him, but somehow I could not do it and sat stiffly as a rod. Neither one of us spoke. The silence was deafening. I suddenly wished I had never had visions of a warm embrace and passionate kisses. Eberhard, also, seemed to have similar problems with self-consciousness, apprehension, and embarrassment. His kiss then caught me by surprise, and I turned my head away slightly so his lips barely touched my cheek. We both got up as if someone had pushed us off the bench, and quickly walked back to the station, chattering in obvious relief, for we had survived our first date.

We both felt that we would be less awkward on our next rendezvous, so we were already planning another one when we walked home from school the next day. But fate, in the form of parish gossips, decided otherwise. We had come too close to my neighborhood before we walked separately, and when I got home, Eberhard's mother was already meeting with my mother in the "grand salon." She left soon without looking at me, and then came the parental showdowns at both homes. We were sternly warned never to be seen holding hands or even walking together again, or we both would be severely punished. We dared not defy all these parental threats, so we avoided each other in order not to endanger one another. Eberhard never dated anyone else, as far as I could tell then, which was a great comfort to me. And I, too, decided that perhaps I was a little too young for dating.

There was a fat, homely, ambitious girl in my class—a teachers' pet thoroughly disliked and distrusted by all of us. The homeroom teacher chose her to be the class representative, but the girl was snitching on us rather than speaking for us.

I decided that any class representative should be elected by the class itself. We held a secret election and sure enough, I was elected to be class leader and representative. I then especially voiced the concerns of the poorer scholars among us if they were unduly or too harshly punished. I also organized "textbook lending," which meant covering up for those who had forgotten to bring their textbook to school. Also, if a girl had a legitimate reason for not having done her homework, I either explained things to the teacher or got her together with our brightest kids just before the onset of classes to help her quickly. If too much homework was piled on us, I organized a class strike or voiced our complaint all the way up to the principal. I even saw to all our physical welfare by collecting funds and sneaking out of school to buy us snacks from a nearby store. We shared these with girls who did not have money, which included me.

The "teacher's pet" faced punishment from a united class if she snitched on us. But just before the end of the school year, while I was absent with a lengthy flu, she got up her nerve to snitch. I almost got expelled from school, but this time my parents—who usually decided that we probably deserved what we got—interfered on my behalf. They had known and approved my concerns for the underdogs in my class (I had especially gotten the class to help defend a Jewish girl who was being nastily discriminated against by several teachers). So my parents now met with the school principal, the fair Dr. Christ. I got off with a

My 1938 class at the Private Lyzeum of East Berlin. (I'm in the second row, fourth from the left.) The anti-Nazi principal, Dr. Christ, is in the top row, fourth from the right.

warning and a reprimand, but I felt hurt and refrained from attending the end-of-the-school year class picnic.

As it turned out, it was not only the end of the school year, but the end of the school! Period! The Nazis, in the early summer of 1938, suddenly decided to close all private schools in Germany, which, of course, included my lyzeum. Hitler's objective was to have the public schools subject all children to more Nazi propaganda, falsified history books, Nazi holiday celebrations, more emphasis on sports, and easier government supervision and spying on teachers.

My parents chose for Odi and me a school in a distant eastern suburb of Berlin called the Richard Wagner *Frauenoberschule*. At least here the principal was not a rabid Nazi, and the tuition was cut in half if a family sent more than one girl there. But before I take us to that new school, let me dwell a little yet on that summer's vacation.

Hans and I were invited for most of the summer to Grandmother and her sister's place in Brieg, near the Polish border by the Oder River, where we had several years ago learned to swim. These two gentle ladies let Hans and me pretty much roam this medieval little town. It featured a large, cool cathedral, thick crumbling city walls, and an old castle. There at one end of the courtyard benches had been set up and one could sit there on weekend nights to watch talented actors perform classic plays about knights and ladies, complete with horses in tournaments. The old castle was all lit up with floodlights and presented a perfect backdrop.

The 100-year anniversary at my great grandfather's birth house in Wilsnak, north Germany. From left to right: Odi, Mother, Father, Aunt Oda (Father's sister), Aunt Olly and her husband, Uncle Siegfried (Father's brother), 1937.

We also roamed the castle park, where a walled-in lake held big, fat, old moss-backed carp. Their mouths were ever open hungrily as we handfed them with stale bread while leaning precariously over the wall.

Swimming in the Oder River and watching an occasional movie kept us busy and happy, also. One film impressed us particularly. It was the sad story of a young cav-

My gentle grandmother Olga Leffler, about 1938.

alry officer who fought bravely against Napoleon and was finally killed. Hans and I cried and sang the theme song. To this day my eyes fill with tears when I hum it.

Speaking about Napoleon, my great grandfather (Father's grandfather)—who was also a Dr. Wilhelm Harnisch—had been one of the founders and leaders of the famous Prussian student conspiracy. He helped form military units under the guise of sports clubs, which eventually defeated Napoleon and chased him out of Prussia. He also (as a young teacher) tutored Princess Charlotte of Prussia. After she had married the tsar of Russia and they had children, she asked my great grandfather to please come to Moscow and tutor her children, which he did for a couple of years. I still have one of her gifts to him—a large tankard made of silver and overlaid with gold. It has several scenes of Moscow engraved on it, and also her signature. A letter of thanks accompanies it, but I only have a copy of it. I don't know what happened to the original.

Anyway, this great grandfather Harnisch became the dean of a famous theological seminary, which was also a teacher's college. He revised textbooks and revamped much

My great grandfather Dr. Wilhelm Harnisch (educator), born in 1837, with his first wife, who died without children.

of the German educational system. He became famous, and I have a copy of his voluminous autobiography, which was published in 1865 and which lacked the last volume because he died. So very much of this man reminds me of Father.

Speaking of Father, I spent the last week of that summer of 1938 on our boat with him. Mother had left Berlin to get some rest at a spa, accompanied by Odi. Hans spent that week riding his beloved horses at Aunt Oda's, and Father finally took one week off. I was elected to cook for him on the boat and to be his companion. We loaded the boat with provisions and Father taught me the rules of boating and how to steer safely, and especially how to handle our tricky engine. Then we left our "cove" and went on an adventure trip. I proudly steered and maneuvered the boat through several lakes while Father slept or read. I had only one close call. A large tanker had entered a narrow lock with us and we slightly collided. I don't know to this day whose fault it was, and it jolted Father right out of the cabin. But miraculously the damage was slight and we were able to continue the trip.

Then I found the lake of our dreams, a hidden, crystal-clear and sky-blue little lake, which had formerly been a chalk mine. You could see the chalk white ledges clearly beneath us, as we successfully anchored there without hitting any of them. We spent several days there. Even Father swam some, and I swam daily to shore, where I climbed around the rocky white cliffs or just laid there and tanned. I cooked meals—per Odi's recipes, not Mother's!—and we spent the nights reading 'til toward morning. I was so proud and happy to have my busy father all to myself for the first and only time in my life.

In the last two to three years while I had grown from a child to a teenager, Hitler's Germany was doing well. He had employed most Germans by building up the army, navy, and airforce, in utter defiance of the Treaty of Versailles. That treaty, signed by the victors and the loser of WWI, had stipulated that Germany would never again arm itself. But a timid world now stood silently by as Hitler built offensive weapons such as tanks, bombers, and U-boats. The world also ignored a pact between fascist Italy and its leader, Mussolini, and Hitler's Germany, which they called the "Axis." And then, in the spring of 1938, Hitler "absorbed" Austria.

Hitler had been a native of Austria, and German-speaking Austria had also been Germany's ally in WWI. My family watched in horror as a wildly enthusiastic Austria greeted the German takeover. And soon there, too, began the persecution of political dissenters, Communists, Jews, Gypsies and dissenting churches, with Austrian police aiding the Gestapo.

The summer of 1938 now saw a growing hate propaganda campaign against Czechoslovakia grow shriller and shriller. Supposedly, the Germans who lived there in an area called the "Sudetenland" were mistreated by the Czech minority. Hitler threatened to invade Czechoslovakia. Now a shocked England and France sent their prime ministers, Chamberlain and Daladier, to reason with Hitler. They met with him in Munich, and as a "compromise" they signed the Munich Treaty with Hitler to let him "liberate" the Sudetenland if he, in turn, would promise not to invade the rest of Czechoslovakia. The very next day, Hitler invaded and "liberated" the Sudetenland, and barely six months later, in March of 1939, he broke the Munich treaty and invaded and conquered Czechoslovakia, where he killed most of its army and imprisoned the rest.

In the years of 1938, 1939, and 1940, Odi and I attended our new school against the backdrop of a fanatic, victory-drunk population, to whom Hitler had become something of a god. I remember the compulsory, flag-swinging, rousing "victory" assemblies in our huge school auditorium, where every student was dressed in the brown BDM uniform. There were only two colorful dresses to be seen in this sea of uniformity: my sister's and mine.

On the home front, too, Hitler and his henchmen increased their evil. By 1939, without the knowledge of most Germans, he had built six concentration camps, including Dachau and Buchenwald. Thousands were tortured and killed there. More and more Jews were rounded up. They had to wear a yellow Star of David in the

> Bonhoeffer's response to the November 9, 1938 pogrom (*Krystallnacht*) reflected his growing conviction of the significance, for Christians, of the persecution of the Jews. In the margin of his Bible, he wrote the date November 10, 1938 (it is the only date marked in his Bible) next to the words of Psalm 74, verse 8: "They said in their hearts, let us plunder their goods! They burn all the houses of God in the land . . . O God, how long is the foe to scoff? How long will the enemy revile your name?"

streets, and in the infamous "crystal night" (so-called because of all the broken windows) almost every Jewish store, establishment, and synagogue in Berlin had been smashed and burned.

One day, on my way home from school, I passed as usual the wired-up glass display box on a building, which I always tried to ignore. It featured several pages of a weekly SS "newspaper" called *The Stürmer* (The Attacker). It was mainly loaded with hate articles against Jews. This day, even I could not ignore it: There was a large, horrible caricature of my father, with a headline screaming "TRAITOR!" And under it you could read that "this preacher Harnisch is an even worse enemy of the Reich than the Jews themselves, because he is a German who champions the Jews."

I came home crying, for we would now again be the target for the Hitler youth and any Nazi fanatic. But, as usual, my parents asked me to ignore the hate and to be brave. And amazingly, there were no consequences for us.

We did manage to save some Jews. There was our family doctor, for whom Father somehow managed to get a fake visa and passport to get him out of the country. And there were German women married to Jews in our parish, whom we helped to cover up and to hide their men. I myself helped to feed a hidden Jewish lady, but one day her place of hiding was ransacked and she was gone.

Generally, the persecution of BK churchmen simmered down, as now the Nazis were mainly busy in rounding up Jews and preparing for more war.

Our new school, the Richard Wagner *Frauenoberschule*, was also a lyzeum, but on top of all the academic subjects we had to learn cooking, gardening, and baby care. I had to take about 12 courses, 80% of which were taught daily. Again, the Nazi teachers gave me rotten marks, regardless of talent or effort, and the few anti-Nazis spoiled me with grades I usually did not deserve.

On opening day in September 1938, I remember being greeted by our new homeroom teacher with the following words: "Ladies! As of this school year, we teachers have to address you all as "Miss" and by your last name. But that does not necessarily mean that you are not a jackass instead of a lady!"

Not long thereafter I incurred her undying hatred. She had required that each of us review and discuss a book of our choice. I chose Dr. Martin Niemöller's *Vom Uboot zur Kanzel* ("From the U-boat to the Pulpit"), with the result that most of the class wanted to read it. Alas—again—no A's for me…

Soon I made friends with a girl who had also freshly entered the school. She was somewhat older than I, and we had few things in common except two important ones: first, she lived halfway along my school route and we could share "el" train rides; and secondly, we were now the two "new rats in the cage" to be sniffed over and then ignored by the rest of the class. So we stuck together.

The way to and from school seemed endless. First a 15-minute walk (run) to the nearest "el" train station called Frankfurter Allee. Then a transfer at the station called Ostkreuz (in the winters it was the coldest of all, because it was open in every direction). Then came a half-hour ride to the final terminal, which was called Friedrichshagen. From there I had another 15-minute walk (run) to school. If I arrived just one minute late, the big portal was locked. One had to ring a bell and was reported as late to the principal. Five such late times per month and one would be expelled from school. I barely hung on.

Odi had a definite advantage over me. She always took earlier trains, because she slept better at night than I did. And she also had entered a much more interesting class than my own. Some of her classmates were even anti-Nazi, and so was her homeroom teacher, an interesting and good-looking man adored by all. Her grades improved drastically as mine sank. I especially hated advanced math with a passion, and once was so petrified of a major exam that I fled from my "el" train on the way to school. I roamed the woods and a deserted racetrack, all the while wondering how I would explain this at home to my parents, who would have to write me an excuse. I finally decided to use "nausea and headache." I got away with it and gained a few days to cram for my make-up exam. Generally I tried hard to follow all rules and regulations and to study hard. But my heart was not in any of it.

We had a tall, gaunt, male music teacher, a fanatic Nazi who tortured the entire school with having to learn endless choirs of Wagnerian operas. Richard Wagner was, of course, Hitler's favorite composer, since his operas featured so often old Germanic sagas, with *Siegfried* and the *Ring of the Niebelungs*. This Mr. W was terribly strict, and kept the entire school's huge choir in terror. But somehow he singled me out to be liked by him, maybe because of my good voice. One day, when I was about 14, he caught up with me as I walked the shortcut through the park on my way back to the "el" station. He escorted me to a secluded bench to discuss something of importance with me. There he suddenly took my face into his hands and tried to kiss me. I dared not hit him or "run for the nearest cops" as my parents had advised me. But I pressed my lips tightly together and twisted away. Then I stuttered—not daring to look into his piercing, passionate eyes—that I did not love him, and that, perhaps, we should both try to forget this. He contained his fury, but made me promise to keep quiet, and then he let me go. I never did tell anyone for fear that I would be accused of having tempted him (he was a married man), or of having to endure his denials and wrath. But I was scared to death of him from then on, although he totally ignored me now.

I still had no idea what sex was all about. Mother was almost hysterical in her denial of sex as a normal part of life. She warned me constantly of most men being animals and of being evil, and never to let any male get too close. No one explained sex to me until I was nearly married, and the school taught me how to handle a baby, but not how to get one. As it was, none of this bothered me too much. I was still something of a tomboy at age 14 and even 15, happy to be bicycling with Hans and his various friends, who were mostly younger than I was.

My more mature girlfriend, Ursula, did not bring up the subject either, but she was long dating older boys, and so was Odi, but secretly.

One day Ursula asked me to accompany her after school on a wooded path, which ran alongside the tracks of our "el" train. There she was meeting a new boy, but was worried a little to be alone with him right away. Being always willing and ready to protect anyone who needed me, I consented and walked along with the two of them until she felt comfortable. Then I rushed back to the station and caught the next "el". When I arrived at our apartment door and rang twice as usual (to identify myself), Father himself opened the door and, without a word, slapped my face hard. Then he withdrew to his study. Stunned and outraged I confronted my sister. Sure enough, she had seen me—from the windows of her "el"—with a boy in the

Odi labeled this photo "The virtuous pastor's kids."
Odi age 16, Gisela 14, Hans 12 (1939).

woods, and she had considered it to be her duty to inform my parents. I called Ursula and she explained the true situation to Father. But no one ever really apologized to me. I was simply told by Father to accept that slap for some other occasion instead, when I would have deserved it.

In crowded subways or at the zoo, sometimes fat old men would press themselves against my back, or would whisper weird words into my ears, which I did not understand. I hated and escaped them, but was never quite sure what they wanted from me. Yet I did enjoy it now when boys gave me admiring looks or whistled as I walked by.

At the end of my 1939 summer vacation—which I had spent with various relatives—Hitler stunned the country and the world by signing a non-aggression pact with Joseph Stalin. Even his own Nazi party was surprised, because they had until then been telling everyone how evil the Communists were, and they had arrested them by the hundreds. But soon we all had the explanation. Stalin knew of Hitler's plan to invade Poland, which he himself had always eyed hungrily. So these two punks closed ranks, and when Hitler on September 1 now—in a Blitzkrieg— grabbed the western half of Poland, Stalin not only let him do it, but on September 17 he himself swallowed up the eastern half of Poland. This was too much for the West. On September 3, 1939, England, France, and Canada formed the Alliance and declared war on Germany. It was "the quiet war" for a while. France moved its troops and supplies to the Maginot Line, while the Germans manned the Siegfried Line. England and Canada moved their troops into France.

Hitler now took time in the winter of 1939 to 1940 to execute Poles. He built concentration camps in Poland and Czechoslovakia for prisoners of war and Jews. And he continued to build up his armed forces.

Then, in April 1940, Germany invaded Denmark and Norway, giving Hitler complete control of the North Sea and perfect hiding places for his fleet. His U-boats now roamed the oceans, destroying merchant vessels everywhere. On May 10, an exasperated England elected Winston Churchill as Prime Minister. On that very day, Germany grabbed Luxembourg and the Netherlands in a five-day Blitzkrieg, and on May 10 headed for Belgium. The Allies now raced from France to Belgium, but Germany reached the English Channel first by May 28, nearly surrounding the allied forces. Belgium's King Leopold surrendered. Britain managed to evacuate most of its troops back to England from Dunkirk, but many were killed, and the remaining allied troops were forced to surrender to the Germans.

The horror continued, to the jubilance of most Germans, Italians and Austrians. Soon thereafter, Japan also joined the fascists, and the pact was now called the Rome-Berlin-Tokyo Axis. Italy declared war on England and France on June 10, 1940.

On June 5, 1940 (my fifteenth birthday), Hitler launched a major assault on France, and victorious German troops marched into Paris on June 14 while the Vichy government fled to the south of France. Hitler signed an armistice with that government, promising to stay out of southern France. This treaty, too, he broke later in 1942.

On July 10, the maniac Hitler started his air war against England. By September 1940 he thought he had destroyed the RAF and he now bombarded London.

There was nothing anyone could do to prevent these horrors. We just prayed that someone, somewhere would stop this Hun and his hordes. And we watched sadly as thousands of singing, confident young soldiers left our city in long troop trains in every direction, cheered on by the masses with flowers and kisses. We knew in our hearts that there would be a horrible end, but even we did not foresee the entire world disaster.

In the spring of 1940 my spelunking friend of my broken-arm-vacation showed up in Berlin. Hansjörg had moved here from Stuttgart. He was in uniform, like most young men were now, but he was permitted to continue his engineering studies in the army because he had too many health problems to be sent to the front.

I was not especially overjoyed to see him, but after a lengthy talk with my parents he was allowed to take me out to operas and restaurants and elegant shops in the west of Berlin. His pedantic behavior, though, spoiled my fun, and I tried in vain to get him to stop making me act like a well-behaved grownup at all times. I was just about to snub him completely, when his parents—the clergy couple in Stuttgart—invited me for that summer's vacation. I had seen and admired Stuttgart from trains, so I accepted gladly.

And it was a lovely city, nestled into a sunny valley, climbing up its hills. The apartment buildings were lighter here than in Berlin, and the people much more relaxed. A charming castle and opera house were quite near the railroad station, where my hosts were awaiting me. A yellow, clanging streetcar took us to the quiet street in a nice residential section just west of the center of Stuttgart, where their large and comfortable apartment was waiting for us.

It was the first time I was spending an entire seven-week summer vacation unaccompanied by anyone from home. I was 15 and feeling quite grown up, especially since Mother had finally let me buy a pair of heeled, strapped summer shoes.

My hosts were somewhat older than my parents. Pastor D's title was *Kirchenrat,* (church counselor). He preached only rarely, as his main function was that of director of a large Lutheran House of Deaconesses. The inhabitants were women of all ages who had forsaken marriage and children to be trained as registered nurses in Lutheran hospitals or homes for the aged, or as teachers in Lutheran kindergartens, and so on. Pastor D, though a member of the BK, seemed to be championing the "good life" rather than the struggle of the BK churches. In fact he shocked and angered me once when he remarked that "Berlin clergymen are rabble-rousers, sticking their necks out too far and making trouble for the rest of us."

He was a ruddy, heavy-set man, with jowls and bushy eyebrows. His favorite, most frequent pastimes were good meals, good wines and cigars, long naps, long nature hikes, and dominating his family. His wife was as quiet and frail as her husband was noisy and robust. She was, with the help of a live-in maid, a marvelous cook, a devoted mother, and the sister of the withdrawn Pastor G of the summer of my broken arm.

None of their three "boys" were at home that summer. Hansjörg was in Berlin, his younger brother Fritz, 22, was a student of theology, drafted into the army. His older brother Walter, age 25, was a medical student who was doing his internship in a military hospital. I was shown so many family photographs and albums that I began to suspect that they were hoping I would join their family, perhaps by marrying Hansjörg, but then I rejected the thought and decided that they were probably just seeing a daughter in me.

They took me everywhere, including the lovely medieval villages and towns around Stuttgart where I was welcomed by several of their relatives. They bathed with me in the warm bubbly waters of the Cannstadt Spa, and we went on long hikes in the grandly beautiful Black Forest. Hansjörg came to visit for a week, and he accompanied me on the piano as I sang Schubert's "The Trout" and "The Mill." My hostess spoiled us all with heavenly meals, served formally by the maid. I always preferred south German cooking anyway to the much simpler north German recipes.

Time flew, and I returned reluctantly to my drab east Berlin and my hated school. Hans looked at me somewhat concerned as I kept on raving to him about the "easy life down south." He could feel my growing rebellion and sensed the danger of separation.

It was now the fall and winter of 1940. The Italians had overrun the few British troops in Somalia. England fought the Italians and then the Germans in northern Africa, where the war continued to seesaw between Rommels *Afrikacorps* and British troops led by Montgomery. Paris was suffering under Nazi occupation, London was being bombed, U-boats were hunting allied shipping, and Hitler busied himself with building and filling concentration camps as fast as possible, along with getting arms and troops ready for his coming spring invasions.

By now, Germans were totally convinced that they were infallible. They saw the Axis as the superpowers that would rule the world forever. Daily, air and sea "aces" were crowned as new national heroes.

In Berlin, three huge anti-aircraft bunker-type towers were being built, one of them quite close to us. And, although Göring had promised no bombs would ever fall on Berlin, some industry was being moved out of the city, as well as some schools.

Because my school was located far out in an eastern suburb, a boys' gymnasium was moved to us from the inner city. It was not being totally integrated with us, of course, because schools of higher learning never mixed genders. Instead, the boys started with their classes when ours ended. Right away, the boys left little notes on their desks to whatever girls occupied those desks in the morning. Most girls responded and dating began between "desk-mates." I read my notes but did not respond to them. Suddenly a boy approached me as I was walking toward my "el" station. It seemed that some girls had pointed me out as his "desk-mate." He was tall and nice-looking, but seemed depressed. He asked me for a date, but I declined. His notes on my desk now became longer and more urgent.

Some were poems of adoration, others accused me of snobbing him, one even hinted about harming himself if I continued to ignore him. I finally wrote him a letter in which I pointed out that there was nothing wrong with him, I simply did not feel like dating and would he please concentrate on someone else. The notes stopped. A few days later the news spread through my school like wildfire—he had committed suicide! His parents called my parents. He had left me a note that my refusal had been the last and final proof of his undesirability. No one blamed me, and it was decided that no one else should see that note. I felt awful, although both his parents and mine assured me that his paranoia would probably have caused his death sooner or later anyway. But I kept wishing I could have saved him somehow.

A heavy load of homework kept me very busy, but I still tried to help Hans with his. It was a sacrifice, because his little room smelled awful. He hated his "out-of-control" bushy and curly hair, and he greased it with some vile-smelling stuff and pressed it down with a tight cap while he slept. Opening a window never occurred to him, either. We all were constantly aware and relieved that Hans was only in his early teens and not eligible for the draft. Quite a few of our acquaintances had already been killed, and we simply could not imagine that Hitler would continue his insane wars much longer.

Hansjörg kept showing up whenever he had a day off, and in November he asked my parents if they would permit me to spend Christmas at his parents' home in Stuttgart. It posed a dilemma for me and my parents, since none of us children had ever spent Christmas away from home. But we finally decided I would go, if for no other reason than to spend my three-week Christmas vacation away from Berlin.

This time Hansjörg accompanied me on my long all-night train trip to Stuttgart. But he made a mistake. He introduced me to an engineering classmate, Helmut Bott, who traveled with us on his way to Wildbad in the Black Forest, where his mother and married brother ran their own resort hotel. Helmut was the most handsome man I had ever seen, though he was almost too tall for many people's taste. He was also a lieutenant in a tank-repair division, ready to graduate in the spring with an engineering degree. We spent most of the night in front of the compartment where Hansjörg was sleeping, talking and watching the stars. When we finally joined Hansjörg toward morning to get some sleep, I fell asleep with my hand resting against Helmut's chest. A peeved Hansjörg woke us up in Stuttgart, from where Helmut went on to Wildbad.

My Christmas vacation with my summer hosts was interesting, to say the least. All three boys were home for Christmas. I now met Fritz, the youngest (drafted theology student), who had a slight bullet wound in his leg, and spent most of the days resting on a couch and reading. I thought he was rather boyish looking and quite shy. He seldom smiled. I sometimes kept him company by playing checkers or other games with him. It seemed to me that he was as intimidated by his father as his mother was.

On Christmas Eve the older brother, Walter (the doctor) appeared. He had finished his internship and was now a full-fledged physician, also in the army and slated to be leaving for Paris after New Year's Day. He seemed somewhat older than his 25 years, but maybe that was due to behavior rather than to facial features. He was friendly but slightly condescending. His main hobby was painting and sketching, and he was really good at it. He asked me to sit for a portrait for him, and I spent many hours not moving while he used soft, pastel chalks to create a life-sized, full-length portrait of me. It was then hung over the grand piano, where Hansjörg again accompanied me as I sang classical arias for the family and guests.

Their Christmas tree was elegant and simple compared to our colorful one at home. I missed especially Hans, but I was kept too busy to have much time for homesickness. There were those wonderful cookie recipes that I gathered from the hostess and the maid. And the meals were a steady delight. We visited many of their relatives again. The Ds were a huge and loyal clan, and my host was the undisputed leader of the tribe. Of interest to me was mainly a male cousin of the "boys," an also-drafted young history teacher, who was planning to become a professor of history. He and Hansjörg and Walter took me on historical excursions through the city and surrounding area.

For Stuttgart's usually mild climate, that winter was rather severe. I had brought my figure skates, and Hansjörg and Walter took me skating to a pretty rink on one of the hills above Stuttgart. It turned out that neither one of them was a good skater. A loudspeaker above the rink sounded Strauss waltzes. I began to dance by myself when a well-dressed, tall male skater asked me to dance with him. I gladly consented and we waltzed beautifully together, in an easy, flowing rhythm. I was totally absorbed, exhilarated and ecstatic. We danced on and on to the great Strauss melodies, neither one of us tiring. When the music stopped I faced two grim escorts who had already removed their skates. In silence we left the rink. I tried in vain to resume the snowball fight we had started before we skated, but there was little response. At home, they tattled to Papa, who took me aside and—knitting his bushy eyebrows together—scolded me for having shown bad manners and bad judgment as an "honored guest" in his house! I was flabbergasted. Did they own me? Why was I so suddenly labeled "naughty"? Was it my fault that Hansjörg and Walter took me skating when they didn't know how? But I was used to adult unfairness and did my apology routine. Then all was forgiven.

The "boys" had made reservations for themselves and for me at a nightclub for New Year's Eve. Even Fritz limped along. There was a stage show, and we had a table quite close to the stage. I must admit that I enjoyed the attentions of my three gala-uniformed escorts, and I certainly loved the elegant but relaxed atmosphere, especially the amazing feats performed by a noted mind reader. When the latter asked for a member of the audience to come on stage, my three escorts immediately volunteered me! The mind reader came down to me, took me by the hand, and I suddenly found myself in the floodlight on stage, with my three escorts enthusiastically leading the applause. The mind reader performed a series of intricate and amazing mind-reading tricks with me. To this day I wonder how he did it and why he was ninety percent correct in guessing my thoughts, experiences, and family life. But I also wonder to this day if my three companions had cued him ahead of time—though they hotly denied that. Anyway, it all added up to an unforgettable vacation.

Adrift

1941 to 1942

A few days after New Year's I was back in Berlin. Now I met Odi's latest boyfriend, whom she had even introduced to the family. He was a nice young man, whose father owned a chocolate factory in Hamburg. What happiness for Hans and me as we shared in the bounty of beautiful boxes of selected chocolates! Rationing had not set in yet, but items such as chocolates, nylons, coffee and tropical fruits were getting much harder to come by. Besides, we children had been deprived of sweets all our lives, so this sudden chocolate bonanza sent Hans and me into ecstasy. We implored Odi to marry this bringer of gifts, but before too long the two had a falling-out. Alas!

Also during this January of 1941, the world famous Don Cossack Choir had sung in the beautiful dome of Berlin to packed audiences. My parents, who had helped to sponsor their appearance, asked five of the Cossacks to have dinner with us. They also invited a visiting Russian princess, who graciously accepted. Cossacks, as well as nobility, were persecuted by Stalin, and many had fled and lived now in exile. Odi had begged off from the occasion, but Hans and I were asked to partake in the dinner.

My mother, who adored nobility, now extensively coached us two how to curtsy and bow deeply, and how to address a princess and behave in the presence of Her Royal Highness.

The important evening had arrived. Mother and I were dressed to the hilt. She had even lent me a pair of her nylons and a pair of high heels from Odi. Even Father and Hans had donned black suits, and the least impaired of our household helpers had been decked out in something resembling a maid's uniform. The table in the salon had been stretched out to accommodate the 10 of us. It featured the best Bavarian lilac china on the whitest, most starched tablecloth, and a lilac-colored silk band had been slung artfully around platters of fruit and flowers and immense silver candlesticks. All was ready.

Punctually at 7:00 PM the guests arrived in two cars. First the Don Cossacks came upstairs, resplendent in their red dress-uniforms trimmed with fur and their black high boots shining to perfection. They were slim and graceful, and although their German was broken it was understandable.

In the meantime, Mother had taken the elevator down to escort the princess up personally. I think we all did Mother proud as we curtsied and bowed deeply, and as Father graciously kissed the royal lady's hand. We had transformed the waiting room into an anteroom to the salon.

There Hans and I served wine, while the "maid" offered the hors d'oeuvres. At first, everyone was somewhat tongue-tied, but soon the wine and Father's wit relaxed us all. The princess—a stately lady in her fifties—wore a long black lace gown and a tiny silver tiara in her graying hair. She and my parents were soon absorbed in discussing their similar political outlook, while Hans and I plied the Cossacks with questions about Russia and their world travels. Then dinner was served.

While we all enjoyed the food (most of it prepared ahead of time by my sister, and the rest by me and the "maid"), Hans and I begged the five Cossacks to teach us a little how to dance the intricate dances of their homeland by the Don River. They laughed and looked at my parents. Mother seemed a little concerned, but Father and the princess smiled.

As soon as my parents and Her Royal Highness had made themselves comfortable in Father's study and had shut the door behind them, one of the guests began to play the greatest Cossack dance music on my grand piano, while the rest of them showed Hans and me some of their intricate steps, splits, and joyful leaps. With the connecting sliding doors to the waiting room wide open we had lots of space. I remember the chandelier shaking and glistening in all its rainbow-hued splendor as we danced, laughed, and sang. Our parents and the princess came out of the study for a while to watch us and applaud. Time had stood still suddenly as we frolicked in our little oasis and forgot all about the deadly desert around us.

The school now made my class do a six-week "practicum" in a pediatric hospital of our choice, to practice what we had learned about baby care, and to gain experience with sick children. Frankly, I think this was just another way for the Nazis to fill in for RNs, because so many of them had been drafted for military hospitals.

The closest children's hospital to our apartment was one in north Berlin—an industrial area even more drab than the east. I had to be there by 7:00 AM daily, which meant getting up at 5:30 AM. I ran for the subway in the cold and pitch dark. No lights were allowed to be seen outside anywhere in Germany now because of possible air raids.

The brick hospital was ugly but warm. I was a conscientious "student aide," and I kept a faithful diary about all activities and events there to serve as a basis for an essay, which we were to turn in to the teacher at the end of the six weeks. My essay was a work of art; lively, interesting and complete with magazine picture clippings about well and sick babies and their needs. But, again, my teacher was a Nazi, and though my family and I expected me to get an A+, the teacher decided that a B- was good enough for me. She even gave me that same B- on my report card, though I had received glowing praise from the nurses and the director of the hospital. Oh well, just another unfair, no-win situation. But my bitterness kept on rising.

Every February, most 15- and 16-year-old "ladies of higher learning" attended a twice-weekly ballroom dancing class in one of several dance studios in West Berlin. These lasted about five weeks and ended with the "grand ball" at the end of March. Odi had attended hers two years earlier, but I had little hope for me because the growing list of war casualties made us feel guilty and uncomfortable about ballroom dancing. Suddenly, Father—whose crippled hip had made dancing for him impossible—decided that Hitler should not have the power to take away all youthful rights, and that life for us three had been scary and tense enough. I was allowed to enroll.

Sometimes Mother, sometimes Odi, sometimes the ever-visiting Hansjörg from Stuttgart would take me there in the evenings and bring me back. It was not safe to walk the streets alone to and from the subways in the pitch-darkness, with air raid sirens now howling occasionally, too. The escort-system was also devised by Mother to be sure I would not start to date any dancing partners.

My first few lessons were productive only in terms of teaching me how to foxtrot. But socially they were a total fizzle, as we were assigned alphabetically to our partners, and the vast majority of the boys of my own age were still much too short for me. For the first time I was beginning to resent my height, of which my family had always made me proud. But then things changed for the better, as the boys were finally allowed to pick their own partners, and a couple of taller ones decided they had enough of short girls, also.

There was especially one good-looking taller boy who singled me out for a lot of attention, to the raised eyebrows of my mother and of Hansjörg, who watched in turns from the sidelines. I was beginning to enjoy myself, though, and tucked away a little volume of poetry he pressed into my hand. It even had an adoring dedication on the inside from my admirer. I fell in love more with these poems of Rainer Maria Rilke than with the donor, but Mother had frisked my desk, which I now realized she had done right along, and she would have stopped my lessons, had Father not—for once—interfered and overruled her.

Our teachers were a married couple, and she was as trim as her husband was ugly, short, and fat. But he danced as lightly and gracefully as his wife.

Now the great debate began at home about the ball gown I would be needing for the grand finale. Odi had designed and sketched a lovely gown for me, and to my great relief I was allowed to choose and purchase my own material so the parish seamstress could make the gown. I decided on a raspberry-pastel colored material, which was of high gloss on one side and non-glossy on the other. I had, of course, the glossy side in mind, determined to look like (a pigtailed) Marlene Dietrich. To my bitter disappointment the entire family voted against the glossy side, even Hans and my usually always-agreeing grandmother. The only compromise I achieved was that the wide sash around my waist, which flowed from there all the way to my feet, would be allowed to shine.

In the meantime, my ladylike, pretty sister Odi—who, by the way, also had to wear pigtails yet—met Helmut Bott, the gorgeous young officer I had met through Hansjörg on the train to Stuttgart. He had actually come to see me again, but Hansjörg guarded me jealously against all newcomers, and I had to admit that Odi was certainly of a more suitable age for Helmut, since she was almost 18 and he was 23. She was stunned by his looks and his quiet manliness and intelligence. He was nearly a head taller than she, but she, too, had experienced problems with finding tall males. They made a lovely couple as they now started dating.

Helmut was to escort her to my ball, because she had access to it as a former student in that studio. And I was allowed to bring two guests. Those tickets were quickly snapped up by my mother and Hansjörg.

The great evening arrived, and the five of us ascended the white marble staircase of a noted hotel in the west, which led to the huge, festive ballroom. Individually re-served white tables with roses and refreshments lined the walls. A tuxedoed orchestra played beautiful foxtrots, pol-kas, tangos, waltzes and slow waltzes, which most of us had mastered by now. I was aware that I looked beautiful, and I was grateful now that I was not glossy all over. Hansjörg and Helmut and my dance class admirer and some other boys now danced with Odi and me, while Mother sipped fruit punch and enjoyed watching her dancing daughters.

Gisela at age 16 in 1941

Then a popularity contest was announced by our teachers. All males were given gilded fans to present, one at a time, to a young woman when they cut in to dance with her during a 10-minute dance potpourri. When the gong rang to end the dancing, the women were to count their fans, and the one with the most fans would be crowned as "Queen of the Ball." The women, also, would choose a king by presenting a young man of their choosing with a gilded chain.

The queen contest began and I never, ever went through such a hectic 10 minutes again in my entire life! Evidently, Helmut, Hansjörg, my admirer, and several other males had decided to do everything in their power to make me queen. They cut in on each other in rapid succession, and somehow the whole thing caught on and males from everywhere joined the dances with me, to be in on the fun. When the gong sounded, Mother had amassed over 100 fans in front of her for me. And my flabbergasted teachers now assured me, that never in the history of this studio, had any queen ever assembled such a huge amount of fans.

After the king was duly chosen in the next 10-minute contest, we were then crowned to deafening applause. We had to dance together now, alone on the huge ballroom floor, with all eyes upon us. Luckily, the orchestra played a slow waltz that was my absolute favorite dance, and neither the king nor I made a single mistake.

Then the king had to dance with the lady teacher, and I with her husband, the four of us alone on the floor. There was only one problem: the orchestra played a tango, which required long steps all the way between one's partner's legs, and, as I had mentioned before, he was very short and squat. But somehow, that, too, passed, without anyone laughing. I must admit I was very relieved when the general dancing resumed, and attention went off me somewhat. I absolutely glowed with pride and exhilaration now, and my many contest-partners were grinning all over. I even liked Hansjörg for that one evening.

All too soon the ball was over. But the memories still make my sister and me smile to this day.

In Berlin, RAF air raids were not too frequent yet, but we were scared like everyone else when the sirens started to wail, usually in the middle of the night. Shaking with fatigue and fear we all would dress quickly, each of us grabbing a small suitcase with silver, jewelry, important papers, biscuits, water, and extra clothing. Mother would shout over and over sarcastically, "Heil Hitler!" and we would grin but beg her to "tone it down, please!" as we headed for the cellar. There we huddled with other frightened tenants, praying or trying to sleep until the end of the alarm was signaled by the now steady tone of the siren. One night when I returned to my room, I first saw the big tear in my blackout shade, and then the jagged fragment of an anti-aircraft shell on my bed.

Hansjörg, who had stopped by for an evening again, asked me to walk with him on his way to the subway. There, in the pitch dark and quiet of the blacked-out city, he proposed marriage to me! I was mute with shock, my thoughts racing how to turn him down without hurting his feelings. I barely listened to his assurances that, of course, I was much too young (not even 16 yet), and that "we" would wait with the engagement. He had loved me since he first met me as a 12-year-old in the village Nabern. He had transferred all his studies to Berlin only to be near me. He went on and on urgently, and then asked me if he had a chance for my yes, either now or sometime in the future.

Throughout his speech I was grateful for the blackout so he could not see my horrified face. And now, with all the tact my parents had taught me, I assured him that he was a nice guy and had been a valued friend, but that I simply could or would never love him, and that we should not see much of each other anymore to spare him pain. I ended up by saying, "Good bye, my friend." And to emphasize the word "friend" I quickly brushed my lips against his cheek and walked away.

When I arrived at home a few minutes later, my parents asked me smilingly if I had consented to become Hansjörg's bride eventually. I was stunned that they all had discussed this ahead of time. Well, at least they now honored my refusal. Shortly thereafter the sirens sounded, and at the same time Hansjörg showed up! He had walked around in the neighborhood to think, and had decided that my kiss was an encouraging sign for him! I was especially infuriated that he now told my parents that I had "kissed him," which meant I either "loved him or was toying with his affections." I quickly explained to my parents that it had been simply a tact kiss, and then I hissed at Hansjörg all the way down the stairs and into the cellar that he was a jerk, that I had no loving feelings but only disgust for him, and to stay away. Period!

That did it. When the sirens signaled the end of the alarm he was gone. Finis! I felt as if a suffocating prison guard had finally been removed. And Hans was happy too, of course.

Throughout this winter and spring I had dragged especially unhappily to and from school. Odi was cramming for her finals—the dreaded Abitur—which she passed to everyone's relief. Hans was suffering in his "Grey Cloister," and I was thinking about informing my parents that I "had enough." Suddenly, at the end of the term, my principal called me into her office and informed me, not unkindly, that she had to warn me that new Nazi regulations would forbid non-members of the BDM or HJ to take the Abitur. And in case I wanted to leave school early, I could do so at any time from now on, without a punitive scholastic record. I never thought that my parents would let me quit so suddenly and so soon, but to my amazement Father was happy I was still unwilling to join the BDM and he agreed I could quit now, since "an education is not as important for girls as it is for boys, anyway." My relief was so overwhelming that on my last day of school at the end of the term I took a run for the almost waist-high wall that girded the schoolyard, and I jumped it and landed on the sidewalk without a tumble!

Shortly thereafter, a pain that I had felt for a long time in the right side of my abdomen increased in severity. Tests at the hospital were inconclusive, but it was decided to remove my appendix "just in case." I remember my fear, the choking struggle against the ether, the awakening in a dark bathroom with sandbags pressed on and against my wound, increasing my agony. (This was done in those days to "minimize the size of the scar.") I thought I was presumed dead by the hospital staff, and had been temporarily pushed into a bathroom before being taken to the morgue. I screamed at the top of my lungs now, which brought the nurses running, who explained I had been put there to keep from waking other patients with crying. No painkillers were given, the sandbags stayed on for 24 hours, and then I was finally wheeled into a room, which turned out to have about 20 patients!

Back home, I was permitted to recuperate a few weeks before I had to start a compulsory year of duty, which faced every boy and girl after schooling, regardless of age. This was, of course, another Nazi invention to find workforces to replace those who had been drafted to fight Hitler's wars of conquest. Girls were to serve on farms and boys to build roads such as the Autobahn. Only one privilege softened the situation somewhat: Girls' parents were permitted to pick a farm off a list for their daughters.

I was introduced to a clergy couple who also ran a "farm"—they had chickens for the sale of eggs and meat. And for Odi they chose a baron and his wife, whom Mother had tutored as children. They had a huge farm, but actually were looking for a tutor for their two children ages six and nine and had long asked Mother for Odi's services.

I must admit that getting away from Berlin and bombs for a while, and to get more food in the country than rationing now allowed in the city, did not seem a bad prospect, and, as soon as my sore abdomen allowed, I started my year of duty.

It was also my birthday, and I was just 16. In April, Hitler had invaded Yugoslavia and Greece. Romania had joined the Axis, in order not to be destroyed. With the

Balkans "secured," Hitler now invaded Russia on June 22. We hoped, of course, that he had overreached himself, especially since Axis ally Italy was not doing too well with conquering North Africa, and had to have help from the Germans. But if the German people started to worry, you could not hear anyone express it. All of Göbbel's propaganda downplayed German losses anyway, and the public simply sunned itself in "victories."

The draft had now grabbed 17-year-olds and family men and males in their thirties. Shortages of teachers, farmers, clerks, nurses and doctors were felt everywhere painfully. Most of our former assistants had been drafted, along with Eberhard, my cousin Ulf, and Berthold's older brother, Günther. Helmut, too, had been sent to the Russian front. He corresponded with Odi. Uncle Engbert, (Mother's brother, who had already served in WWI) was sent to Yugoslavia to help repair the smashed electricity works there, while Father's military brother was somewhere in the Netherlands repairing bombed bridges. All 17-year-old parish youths were sent out to war already, and heartbroken parents cried in Father's study. We thanked God daily that Hans was only 14.

The BK clergy couple to whom I would now be sent for my year of duty had also been separated by the draft. They had a two-year-old girl, and another child was on the way. I shortly met the mild, friendly husband while he had a short furlough at home before being sent to Russia. They lived in a small village about 150 miles northeast of Berlin and only 20 miles away from where Odi was tutoring the baron's offspring at their estate.

A huge amount of work awaited me at this old rectory. A large chicken coop had to be searched for eggs by me daily, the chickens then let out and watered and fed, and the coop cleaned. I weeded the garden, scrubbed the stone entrance hall daily with hot soapy water, tended the child, cleaned the whole place and washed the laundry in hot kettles. My room was in the attic, hot in summer and icy in winter. But I loved looking at the storks nest from up there, which graced the top of the steep, red roof of a barn right across from my window. I watched the loyal parents taking turns feeding their young with frogs from a nearby swamp. They greeted each other with heads leaned backwards as their long beaks clattered noisily. And I laughed as I watched the young learning to fly, hopping straight up into the air and beginning to hover over the nest as their wings thrashed wildly. But I had little time to watch them.

While a neighboring old clergyman took over her husband's pastoral duties here, the "lady of the house" did not exert herself unduly. She sewed, cooked, read the Bible, and awaited the arrival of the next little one.

I finally got up my courage to insist that she let me have a few hours off on Saturday and Sunday afternoons. The pain from my appendectomy dragged on, too, because of the heavy straining and lifting. I smiled bitterly when I thought of myself as the "Queen of the Ball," and felt like Cinderella in reverse.

I had brought my bike along, and took one summer Sunday off to visit Odi. The contrast in our year of duty roles was almost ludicrous: she was treated like an honored guest in the mansion of the Baron von Arnim and his lovely wife. Odi always dined with them, which even the children's nanny was not allowed to do. Tutoring the obedient, pretty little kids was not much of a chore either, and Odi had much spare time to roam their park and gardens. The Von Arnims used to spend the off summer days in Berlin, but the air raids made them use their country estate all year round now, and they needed reliable tutors for the children, who were supposed to learn more than one does in a village school. So the baroness had urged my mother to send her Odi.

The gardener there was a French prisoner of war, as were all their farmhands. I saw him just briefly, and he was very handsome. To communicate with a prisoner of war was punishable by death for civilians. But my rebellious sister befriended him and they met nights in the park. She helped him to communicate with his family in France as she took over the correspondence (at least our school French was useful now). I asked few details. I was just proud that she had confided in me. If the von Arnims knew about all this, they kept it to themselves. They hated Hitler as much as we did, and they treated the prisoners, which had been assigned to them, with much kindness and great care.

Shortly thereafter, my pastor's wife had her baby, and I took care of two children now. Then, a few weeks later, a telegram informed her that her husband had been killed in Russia. I will always remember her opening that telegram and starting to scream. She threw herself onto the couch, flailing her arms and legs and screaming, screaming… I grabbed her kids and fled to a neighbor's house, from where we called the stand-in clergyman. He and his wife then took the distraught woman to their house for a week, while I kept the household going.

I had befriended several village children, and they came, with their parent's consent, to help me now. I was truly moved. We scrubbed and sang and cooked, and I asked them all to come on Saturday evening for a "party," and to bring their friends. I decorated the drab parish hall with streamers and brought the record player in there. Some parents sent cookies and fruit punch over. They came in droves, and we had ourselves a wonderful "ball." I had found a few records with foxtrots and polkas, too, and taught my grateful crowd how to dance. Once more in my life, youth and happiness triumphed for fleeting moments.

The winter was particularly hard for me because I had to bring in firewood and drag buckets of coal up from the cellar to keep the stoves going and the house warm. My little room upstairs was barely thawed with a tiny electric heater. Staring at the empty storks' nest did not make me feel any better, either. I wished the birds could have taken me with them to Africa.

On December 7, the Japanese attacked Pearl Harbor. The next day the United States declared war on Japan, and the day after Hitler declared war on the United States. The war was now global, and most of the countries in the world took sides—luckily backing the Allies. In September, already, the Germans had pushed deep into Russia. They had surrounded Leningrad, and that poor city was being blockaded and starved for the next three years. The United States needed some time yet to bolster its forces and train its men, but we knew that all this had signaled the eventual downfall of Hitler. We hoped it would be soon.

Odi, Hans, and I were all home for the holidays. Food was getting scarcer in the big cities, and rationing more severe. A few of my farm "family" friends, whom I had helped to make sausage from pigs as winter approached, had sent meat and lard along with me for my family, which helped to feed us all for the holidays. Only too soon did I have to return to my "duty."

Odi and Helmut were corresponding, and I suddenly received letters—forwarded to me by my parents at first—from Hansjörg's brother, the doctor Walter. He was still stationed in France somewhere, and hoped to hear from me. He never mentioned Hansjörg, but I assume he knew. His letters were interesting and witty and frequently accompanied by good sketches, including a self-portrait. And then, as belated Christmas presents, I received a bottle of French perfume and a pair of nylons, both of which I saved for future occasions.

I was so depressed in that winter of 1941-42 that this correspondence with Walter helped to cheer me up somewhat. I had definitely liked him better than Hansjörg, anyway.

Another diversion was skating. I had brought my figure skates with me from Berlin, and to my delight the big lake near the village had totally frozen over. Since I rarely had time to skate during the day I skated mainly late in the evenings whenever the moon shone brightly. It was a wondrous experience. The lake was surrounded with a snow-laden conifer forest. Since it had luckily frozen over on calm days and nights, its surface was smooth. It was so cold that an occasional boom startled one, as the ice contracted and cracked slightly. An unlucky deer had been frozen in while crossing, and only it's back stuck out of the ice. After my initial sadness I used it to make practice jumps over it. Skating there all by myself, on that huge white expanse, was one of the most exhilarating experiences of my life. I raced, jumped, waltzed, glided softly and even sang. Eventually a village boy had espied me and brought his skates. I did not mind. He was strong and harmless and we chased each other and yelled to our hearts' content. I paid for this late frolicking with weariness the next day, and I dragged through my chores, but it was well worth it.

The storks came back in the spring and I greeted their return as a sign of hope for myself. The old house started to warm up, too, and I was now counting the days to May and the end of my stay there. But I had a near disaster. Some of the farmers had let me ride one of their horses occasionally. I liked one in particular, a dark brown handsome gelding. I always rode alone, since no one else there was interested in riding.

One sunny Sunday afternoon in April the gelding and I set out together. As I rode through the greening fields and blossom-filled orchards I thought of the lovely poem by Rilke, *"Reitvorschriften für eine Geliebte"* ("Riding Instructions For a Beloved"). It had been raining for several days, and my horse and I were glad of the exercise and the fresh air. We came to a large puddle formed in a hollow of the path along the woods. The horse hesitated and I urged him on gently to wade through. He shied, bucked, threw me off, and galloped away, reins dangling. My head had a big lump and I was aching all over. I decided to lie still, in case I had a concussion. I remember looking at the blue sky and some catkin-loaded branches above me, praying that the horse would make it home. He did, and a search party was formed, wherein half the village took part. A couple of little boys heard me first when I yelled. To everyone's relief, and especially to my own, I was bruised and aching, but not seriously hurt, and soon recovered completely. Needless to say, I did not dare to ask for a horse again.

Suddenly, the year of duty was up. I left with barely a "thank you" from the woman whom I had served so unflinchingly and loyally. But my many village friends gave me a little farewell party and gifts, and some of us cried as we parted.

Odi was done, also, and we met in the next small city called Prenzlau, for a few days of R & R. Odi had even been paid by the grateful baroness, so she had reserved a hotel room for the two of us. We wanted to celebrate our

In 1942, at age 17, I was old enough to receive my certificate of
membership in the BK resistance movement.

new freedom and do some shopping and talking and dining before we returned to Berlin.

The hotel alone made me feel civilized again, and the
bed was pure heaven. I had not even felt running warm
water since our Christmas vacation. We had made big plans
for our first full day there, but a tooth began to hurt during

the night, and we headed for a dentist's office instead. Some of my neglected teeth had to be drilled and filled. The lady dentist was gentle, but she evidently had never heard of novocaine. I suddenly found myself on a couch, staring back at the concerned faces of Odi and the dentist, as they were reviving me. After an hour's rest the teeth were finished up and Odi and I could celebrate the end of our year of duty in style now.

When Bombs Decide

1942 to 1943

B ack home I renewed old friendships with a few classmates, swam and biked with Hans, celebrated my 17th birthday, and corresponded occasionally with Walter, who had been sent to work in a field hospital at the Russian front. I helped with household chores, of course, but not too diligently. My parents finally complained that I used my muscles mainly in other people's households. Well, my mind was simply on much more important things, such as what to do with my life.

I was worried about Hans and Odi, too. My sister was presently not as lucky as I. She was already caught again in another net of a Hitler "strategy" because she happened to be "over 18, unmarried, and unemployed." So instead of entering a university to study art, she found herself forced

Odi in 1942, age 19, in East Prussia in the Female Labor Corps on her day off.

into a one-year stint in the paramilitary "Labor Corps." This Nazi institution had formerly consisted mainly of young males whom Hitler used for building his strategic highways and other war projects. Because all young males were in the military now, young women were forced to replace them as a cheap and vital labor force.

Odi was sent immediately to East Prussia, a north German province between Poland and Russia. There she lived in a prison-like barrack, regimented by fanatic Nazi females. Her Corps peers were sent to perform hard labor at various area farms, while Odi, as a lyzeum graduate, was permitted to teach school. Her classes were large because of so many missing teachers.

At summer's end, a scarlet fever epidemic broke out in Odi's barrack. The immune systems of her exhausted "sisters" had gone on strike. And Odi got it, too. Only when she became delirious with raging fevers was she finally moved to a hospital, where she nearly died. With that, her "Labor Corps" duty was ended very prematurely, and she returned to Berlin to recuperate at home. After listening to her tales of horror, I swore to myself that I would do every possible thing in my power to avoid the Corps.

That summer, Hans also got nabbed by Hitler and Company. He was finishing up his spring term in the "Grey Cloister" when the principal assembled his class and informed the boys (all between 14 and 15) that they would not be permitted to return to this school—or any other one, for that matter—in the fall. The three flak (antiaircraft) towers were short on non-shooting military personnel, and every boy in the class at the age of 15 would be drafted into the military to help man these towers. My parents then were sent a copy of the official order.

Hans at age 15, already drafted.

So our worst nightmare had come true: Hans would be drafted! Although he would not be sent out to fight, these antiaircraft towers were obviously a coveted target for bombers. And, even if not hit, life in them would be sheer misery. His education was also over, of course. We asked each other time and again, when would this insanity end?

At the same time, Hitler was also determined to rid all Europe of Jews. From every German-occupied land, trainloads of Jewish families arrived at the various KZs to be gassed by the millions over the next three years. Dr. Martin Niemöller, the outspoken head of our BK, had been a thorn in Hitler's side for years. He, too, was now shipped to Dachau, where he spent years under horrendous conditions until rescued by Americans at the war's end.

Hans was enjoying his last few weeks of freedom yet with his beloved horses at Aunt Oda's. My exhausted father spent three weeks in June at the mountain resort Bad Gastein. And Mother—who had suffered for years now under angina pectoris, which are painful heart spasms—headed for Bad Els, a small spa near the Czech border. I would be her companion and aide, a role which I did not particularly cherish.

Bad Els was a pretty little spa located in a valley surrounded by steep hills, dark-green with pinewoods. But it was also boring, like most spas. The comfort of sick (and rich!) guests was the foremost consideration in a spa, so hotels and guesthouses (quite a bit cheaper) made up the majority of buildings. A well-kept park featured little drinking fountains that spouted the most evil tasting, but "curative," sulfur-based water, which was slowly sipped by strolling guests.

A huge "curehouse" adjoined the park. It was an elegant health facility, where many individual bathrooms had rails on which wooden tubs full of mud rolled in and out, before and after use.

Per Mother's and her doctor's orders I suffered through a few of such "pigs' wallows," as I crassly called these mud baths. Assisted by a female attendant, I climbed into one of those tubs of horror, holding my nose tightly to avoid the pungent stench, and then—with closed eyes—tried not to think about this hot gooey black mess, which covered me completely up to my throat.

Hot mud was considered to be good for arthritis, circulation problems, rheumatism, female woes and many more ailments. What little improvements I could have used myself did not occur, because I simply lacked the faith in the mud. But I admit I loved the attention of the attendants as they then rinsed off my mud with warm and cool waters, wrapped me in huge warmed towels, soothed my skin with fragrant lotions, and relaxed my muscles with a great massage.

We were quartered in a guesthouse that also served all meals. After her morning "treatment" Mother always took a long afternoon nap, during which I was free to go. I usually browsed through boutiques and the library. Or I hiked in the mountains, bringing back some of the prolific wildflowers.

Gisela at the spa, 1942

The park also featured a white bandstand, from where I could hear the strains of some snappy tunes in the afternoons. When I heard my favorite, the "Viennese Serenade," I decided to listen a while. I picked one of the many lounge chairs quite close to the bandstand and watched the band as well as the handsome young conductor, resplendent in his dress uniform. This was a military band of great expertise. As the bandleader faced his audience to acknowledge the applause, our eyes met. I felt sheer admiration for his classical face, and a surge of happiness overcame me as he smiled at me. Had I answered his smile? I wasn't sure as I got up and sauntered away.

I kept thinking of the man all night long, and hoped for what? The next day I couldn't wait for Mother to take her nap and then eagerly headed for the bandstand. They were already playing, and I took the same seat I had occupied the previous day. To my delight he saw me the moment he turned around. This time I knew I was smiling back.

During a pause, a band member handed me a note and waited for my reply. In his message, the "man of my dreams" asked me to please meet him soon after 5:00 PM, the end of the concert. I was able to consent, as Mother had more "curative sessions" at the end of the afternoon. I would have about one half hour of freedom yet. And so we met.

I had known for years now that men found me attractive. It had bolstered my self-esteem, but had never left an impact until this moment. This was different. I, who usually bubbled with witty conversation and charming demeanor, felt suddenly tongue-tied, clumsy, inexperienced and self-conscious. If he noticed my tension he did not react to it. He thanked me for meeting him, and he took my hand as we walked along the many little paths crisscrossing the park. As he told me about himself I began to relax. I still dared not to look at him, but I responded now to the slight pressure of his hand. I told him a little about myself and then we stood still and looked at each other. I studied his handsome features, his black curls peeking from under his cap, and as our eyes met I felt as if I was falling.

At my urging we now hurried back so I would not let Mother wait too long. I promised to meet him at 7:00 PM in two days, as I knew this would be Mother's letter and postcard writing evening.

Then we met as planned. We had dressed casually as also planned, so we could climb up one of those mountains adjoining the park. At a clearing covered with goldenrod we stopped. My heart was pounding so hard that I was sure he could hear it. At first I thought it was hammering due to the steep climb, but then I realized it was pounding because I was so close to my first kiss. I technically knew how to kiss, due to my more experienced girl friends explaining the procedure to me, but I had waited so long to experience it, and I was hungering now.

His arms encircled me and I closed my eyes. In the silence that followed I suddenly heard his voice by my ear, whispering softly, "Please look at me." I did, and he continued, "Tell me truthfully—have you ever been kissed?" I blushed and shook my head. He stepped back a little and said, "My God, I am sorry. I didn't know." I was stunned and asked him why that mattered. I only heard part of his answers through my hurt. I was "too young" and he did not want to "hurt me." He would be "leaving soon" with his band, and I must not "fall in love with him." I deserved "much better men" than him. He walked me down the mountain, while my eyes were stinging with tears I did not want to shed in front of him. Before we parted in the park, he took my face in his hands and said softly, "I won't kiss you because I don't want you. On the contrary, I won't kiss you because I want you too much!" I dimly understood now what he meant. He kissed my hand, saluted and was gone.

I wished I could have left Bad Els now. But there was yet another week to go. Understanding did not really stop the pain, just as one understands, for instance, when a tooth has to be pulled. But that does not ease the pain of the extraction! I avoided the park now and stuck close to Mother.

An article in the local paper caught my eye. It described the pain of loneliness suffered by injured soldiers who were cramming the local hospital from every corner of Europe. And it asked especially young people to visit the wounded.

With Mother's permission I went to the hospital one afternoon, with a bunch of wildflowers I had picked. Someone escorted me to the surgical ward, where a nurse pointed to a bed. I headed straight for it, not wanting to see all the pain around me.

A happy face greeted me. He had only one arm left; both legs and the other arm had been shattered by a grenade. He seemed not much older than 20, and he thanked me for the flowers and bade me to sit on his bed. I looked around now and saw some girls sitting on other beds. Some were kissing, and behind several drawn curtains one could sense activity.

"My" soldier followed my eyes and grinned. I now felt his left (and only) arm working itself under my skirt. I blushed and carefully moved somewhat, but did not have the heart to walk out. We talked quietly for a few minutes and then he began to caress me again on my upper thigh. His voice became urgent and he pleaded. I stood it for a few minutes longer, partly curious and partly trying to act like "an adult." But my distaste got the better of me. While his voice now changed to anger and abuse, I left the room. So this was another kind of male.

The day before we were to leave I was meandering through the town once more. As I was crossing its main boulevard I became aware of people lining it. And then I heard music—HIS music! I stood by the curb, unable to move as the band came closer. It was leaving town, parading and playing proudly to the applause of many spectators. The band was headed for the outlying railroad station, as he led it. And then he saw me. When he was directly in front of me he ordered the band to "halt" and to change the tune. They now played the "Viennese Serenade" as he smiled into my eyes, while tears were beginning to stream down my face. Then I heard the applause come and go. He directed the band to face us all, and then they saluted in unison, as his eyes bored into mine. Now they resumed their parade, rounded a corner with the music fading away and leaving me crying and alone at the curb.

The next day I was back in Berlin, wiser but not happier. Hans's induction, Odi's return, and the rumors of a major defeat of German troops at Stalingrad—where a stubborn Hitler had finally been stopped with horrendous loss of life—brought me back to reality. Even Göbbel's propaganda mill could not ignore the disaster. Hitler had learned nothing from Napoleon's bitter defeat in Russia, and, despite Germany's "victories" everywhere else (Southern France had also been grabbed by Hitler now), the corpses of his best troops at Stalingrad had thinned the fighting ranks, regardless of the merciless draft at home.

My first "date," the shy and lanky Eberhard, had been killed too. His mother joined the other crying women now in Father's study, trying desperately to find solace in prayer and companionship.

Hans was now in uniform, too. He had grown to be a very tall, slender, handsome teen. Of the three of us, he was, without question, the best looking. Few boys' faces could match his even features, huge black eyes, and wavy dark hair. Although uniforms make most males look improved, Hans looked awkward in fatigues and dress uniforms alike. His figure was too boyish yet, and he wore civies at every opportunity, for this and for rebellious reasons.

He had been assigned to the flak tower nearest us. The bombing of Berlin had increased, though our neighborhood had been spared. We were glad that he did not have to shoot at planes, but we were worried that he had to spend every single night on that tower, even when he had the day off.

Reluctantly I decided to start pediatric nurse's training. Odi at least could now attend art classes at the university, but my study and career options were limited. I thought perhaps I should become a deaconess, but my sister warned me that I was not the right type for a selfless, so-cially isolated profession, and would probably want to get married sometime, anyway. So since I had been trained somewhat in baby care already, and since I had found out that I would be very conscientious with the care of sick babies, I enrolled as a student nurse at the Kaiser Wilhelm Children's Hospital in West Berlin.

Mother bought me two nurse's uniforms. I started classes and practical care, made friends with a couple of other student nurses, and spent my long subway trips read-ing pediatric textbooks. The hospital itself was modern but badly understaffed. It was situated nicely between Hans's and my beloved zoo, and the elegant shopping avenue Kurfürsten Damm, called affectionately "Ku-Damm" for short. But being on nightshift every third week kept me too tired to enjoy the outdoor cafes and the shops of the area.

The worst thing about nightshift was, of course, the air raids. The hospital's first floor hallway was stacked high with lined baskets. At the sound of the dreaded howling of the sirens, each staff member grabbed two baskets, bundled two sick babies into them and rushed them downstairs into the cavernous cellar. Then we raced back upstairs (the two elevators were tied up from the upper floors) to bring down more babies. Only when the floor was empty could we ourselves huddle in the cellar. Some nearby explosions made the building shudder, for many more bombs were falling here than in East Berlin.

I did not want to die. Neither did anyone else, of course, but I thought it would be particularly unfair for me and other dissenters to die "for Germany" when we had hated and despised the Nazi dictatorship from the very begin-ning. I felt myself praying (for the rest of the war) like a schizoid mental patient. My prayers would beg God and the RAF to stop the bombing, and at the same time I implored God and the Allies to increase the bombing to defeat the Nazis.

Once, after a night of horror, I was bone-tired on my early morning subway ride home and fell soundly asleep. I did not wake up 'til hours after the train had been stopped and moved onto a siding. I managed to pry open a door and was luckily only a few feet away from the station. After those nights, I was always grateful to find out that at home my family was still alive, and Hans also.

But even during day duty I had trouble concentrating. I felt somehow devoid of "feeling," and the future did not excite me. Being 17 and "grown up" was not quite the fun I had envisioned, especially because I was still living at home, and now without Hans. I was also still hurting from Bad Els. And I was sickened by the lecherous advances of older men, which I had to endure in subways and on the streets. Also, although my job kept me busy, I just simply did not feel the same commitment to it that I sensed in my fellow student nurses.

Walter's letters became more frequent as his field hospital became more endangered somewhere at the Russian front. Then suddenly my parents asked me if I was "interested" in Walter. They told me that he had asked them in writing if they would consent to a "more serious relationship" between me and him, and if they would ask me about "my feelings towards him." It all reminded me rather painfully of his brother Hansjörg's approach, but I promised my parents I would "think about it!"

And I did, adding up meticulously first the pluses and then the minuses of a marriage to Walter.

Pluses for marrying Walter:

1. Since he was from South Germany I would get away from this awful city and its bombs (I knew that my family was thinking along those lines, too!)

 2. He was a medical doctor, and I would enjoy hugely being called "Frau Doktor" (How I could brag with that title, especially to my former classmates and my hated teachers! Wouldn't all those "old maids" be just green with envy!)

3. His family was educated and fond of me. His background would make him an acceptable son-in-law to my parents.

4. He was artistic and seemed to be witty.

5. If I planned the wedding just right, I could beat my sister to the altar!

6. Marriage—or at least motherhood—would shorten my not so happy present career.

7. I could escape the latest Nazi direction to join the "Labor Corps" automatically at age 18, if the wedding would take place on or before that date.

8. He was not bad looking. I studied his self-portrait carefully as I hung it over my bed now. If one overlooked the broken nose and eyeglasses, especially in his resplendent medical officer's uniform, he was quite presentable.

9. He had written me once that he had never been in love. That meant to me that he would be a loyal, rather than an untrustworthy, male.

10. An early marriage would save me from my own nature, which struck me sometimes as too warm, impulsively passionate, and much too trusting. I could also feel my parents' worry that I might soon be dating the "wrong kind of man."

11. And last, but not least, I would finally be "free" of this very parental supervision.

Minuses for marrying Walter:

1. I did not really know this man "from Adam"!
2. I had not really had a chance to try "a few other dates."
3. He was one inch shorter than I (but that could be fixed with higher heels).
4. He was a far cry from a movie idol (but at least I would not have to worry about constant female competition).
5. My feelings for him were not LOVE. (But I suppose love often comes with marriage).
6. He was ten years older than I (but his wisdom might be useful to me).

After juggling a lot more of the pros and cons, I decided that the pros outweighed the cons.

My parents and Odi were pleased about my consent, but deep down I was even more leery about the whole thing than Hans was.

I added my consenting letter to that of my parents. Walter now sent more letters, sketches, and poems than ever. We also planned to become officially engaged as soon as he could wrangle a furlough, which he did for October since he could get five days off then. We planned to meet at his parents' place in Stuttgart.

When I arrived at the Stuttgart train station he was already there and waiting, resplendent in his best dress-uniform. But with him waiting were his "papa" and "mama"...

As soon as I had unpacked and freshened up, Walter asked me to go for a walk with him. He led me to nearby Silberburg Park, which had once been part of a private estate and still featured exotic plants and fruit trees. A deserted villa could be seen from the distance.

There, under an ancient oak, he put a golden ring on my hand and kissed me gently on my lips. We were engaged.

That was it? I suddenly felt like mocking him, getting him to drop his stiff posture. Or was I just escaping from my own embarrassment and self-doubt? I think today that it was probably both. Anyway, I started to run. "Catch me," I laughed, though I knew full well that he could not do that, if only for the length of his decorative sword hanging from his side. I ran a wide circle and arrived back at the oak. By the time he had caught up with me I had climbed into the upper branches of the tree and pelted him now with acorns. When I saw his face tightening I suddenly thought of the skating rink two years ago…

Gisela Harnisch (age 17) and Dr. Walter Dölker (age 27) engaged.

I forced a "please" from him before I finally came down. He tried to save face by telling me how he "loved my youthful exuberance." And later on he tried once more to convince me that he found my rude behavior quaint by making a crayon sketch of the entire ridiculous scene.

The five days flew by. Each uncle and aunt had to be visited, and all looked forward to my joining the clan. Only Hansjörg was noticeably absent, and young Fritz was on a battlefield somewhere...

Walter painted and sketched, and I ate "Mama's" good cookies. Somehow it all seemed not much different from the two vacations I had spent there, the main exception being the discussion of the wedding plans. We all agreed that the goal should be my 18th birthday in June, should Walter be able to get furlough for it. The place should be Berlin, and lists were already being drawn up for the various relatives who would travel there.

Then Walter was back in Russia and I was back in Berlin and in my nursing student's uniform.

During the winter of 1942 and the spring of 1943 the enthusiasm about victories and war began to tone down in Germany. Even the most fanatic Nazis looked grimmer now as United States bombers had joined the RAF in hitting Berlin and all major German cities. Food lines were getting longer, especially in the early morning to get a hold of a better piece of fish or meat.

There were many other signs of the war having been stalled or even turned. There were the huge losses on all sides in Africa. The Americans had landed in Algeria in November, and Patton had now become wise to Rommel's hit-and-run strategies and was beating the Germans in tank battles. London had cracked many of the Nazi's most secret codes without their catching on to it. In Berlin, less and less khaki-clad soldiers of the Africa Corps could be seen on furlough. And on February 2, the last of the German troops surrendered to the Russians at Stalingrad.

Göbbel's propaganda machine was still cranking out the *Wochenschau* ("Weekly Review"), which was a preamble to any film in any movie theater. It still featured "victories" at sea and in the air or even on land, but whispers about losses and the growing lists of the dead and missing and seriously wounded, the hunger starting now, and the ruins and fear growing in the cities made the *Wochenschau* now look like the farce it was. But to doubt the war successes openly was punishable by imprisonment or worse, and there were spying eyes and ears everywhere.

On his few days off, Hans came home and frequently brought some of his best buddies with him. If I was free at the same time I helped to feed this ever-hungry crowd. All of them were too young to be dating yet, and we let them sleep off their exhaustion or played board games or talked about their messed-up lives. Hans and I even rode our bikes yet a few times, but somehow we had lost our "lust for life." Apprehension and outright fear, though seldom expressed, was our escort at all times.

Besides seeing Hans occasionally, there were a few other highlights for me during that winter and early spring. One of them was my only trip back to my last school, for the sole purpose of bragging with my ring and engagement pictures. I absolutely inhaled the sour and envious "Congratulations!" from the various nasty maiden teachers, who had made my life so miserable there.

Odi and Helmut were dating whenever he was in Berlin. She majored in art at the university and insisted on my modeling for her in the nude. I finally consented, but only behind the locked bathroom door, and under the oath that she would not show the sketches anywhere except in her class. I must admit that I was impressed with her skill as well as with my own slender, long-legged figure.

Odi had finally cut her pigtails and braved my parents' "disappointment." But I—at 17 and engaged—was still stuck with them. Suddenly an idea struck me. I piled all my hair on top of my head in an "up-sweep" for a couple of weeks. Then I took a deep breath and, at a beauty parlor far from parish eyes, had it cut. The hairdresser colluded with me and teased it and piled it back up on top of my head, so it looked almost as full as before. With trepidation I casually walked around at home, and to my great relief no one was the wiser. It was several weeks before Mother caught me brushing and teasing my short hair one day, and since the "proof was in the pudding" that I looked the same as always, my parents kept their disappointment to a minimum. And as I had once been Cinderella in reverse, I was now Samson in reverse...

In March, Walter's letters suddenly stopped. Then I got a phone call from his parents that he had been wounded, but it was not life-threatening. He had been transported to the army hospital in Schwäbisch-Gmünd, a small town about 50 miles east of Stuttgart. I soon heard from Walter himself. He advised me not to travel to him yet. He had decided to accept a position as a staff doctor at that hospital, and as soon as he was ambulatory he would look for us for an apartment in that town, which would be readied for our occupancy in June. To all our surprise, he did manage to find an apartment there, which was quite an accomplishment in view of the fact that the bombing of the cities had resulted in a steady stream of people taking up residences in the safer small towns.

In March 1943 I now took the train first to Stuttgart and then a smaller commuter train from there to Schwäbisch-Gmünd. And I fell in love with this charming, medieval town at first sight. Especially the center of Gmünd could have been taken right out of a pictured storybook. The three churches there span Romanic, Gothic, and

The Schwäbisch-Gmünd marketplace

Baroque eras. I loved those ugly little gargoyles on the huge gothic dome, as they leered down onto the little houses crowded below. The market place, complete with an ornate fountain surrounding a front-and-rear facing Madonna, could only be distinguished from medieval eras by modern cars and attires. I marveled at the pastel-colored facades of half-timbered little shops and inns and the town hall framing this market place. At one end, a stone arch above the street connected directly to the hospital, where my fiancé was now staff physician. The opposite end of the market oval led via narrow alleys to a stately ancient watchtower, from where steep stairs led up the hill directly to the street and the parish house.

This rectory was an imposing yellow, two-storied concrete building. It was a double house, where each side had its own entrance. The two top floors were clergy residences, and the two first floors were their three-room offices with washrooms. The right side of the house was occupied by the only local Lutheran pastor, T. He was a stout member of the BK, a kind, white-haired tall man, whose devoted wife and five well-behaved children made up his family.

On the left top floor resided Dr. Asmussen, a leading BK clergyman from Berlin, who had fled from the bombs with his British-born wife and two teenage children. The empty three-room office below was being readied for our occupancy after our wedding in Berlin in June. It was evident that Walter's influential "Papa" from Stuttgart had much influence with the Lutheran church of Gmünd to let his son have that apartment.

During the week of my visit I was a guest of Pastor T's family. The five children took me immediately under their wings. They proudly showed me their lovely town. We also hiked up and down the mountains, which started at the end of their curvy, broad, steep street. These mountains are part of a chain called the Schwäbische Alp. Several of the mountains feature ruins of ancient castles, which I explored with the children of my kind hosts and with my fiancé.

Walter's shoulder wound had sufficiently healed now to permit him almost complete use of his left arm. He was an internal specialist and had not been sufficiently trained as a surgeon. He and almost all German physicians had been pressed into performing surgery because of the countless war-wounded. Despite his experience in various field hospitals at the front, he needed to bone up, as well as practice, in the OR. There he worked under the guidance of the chief surgeon, Dr. Finger, an ill-humored, arrogant, highly-ranked man of great skill. Walter and I had little time to ourselves under these circumstances.

All of his needs were taken care of by the hospital. Better than average meals were served to the physicians in their own dining room. His laundry was also taken care of, and he resided in a very comfortable private room. The hospital had been a Roman Catholic facility before the military took it over. The nurses—all of them nuns—stayed on, tending to the many wounded soldiers who crowded the facilities and aiding the doctors in the four operating rooms.

I got along well with his fellow army physicians, who made me feel at home as soon as I arrived. And since they knew that my civilian food ration card did not satisfy anyone's sweet tooth, they took turns saving all kinds of desserts and sweets for me.

There were no intimacies between Walter and me. Much later I found out that my parents had made him promise that he would keep my "virginity intact" 'til the wedding. And to Walter that meant not even kissing! I admired his many skills, but I felt little desire to be touched by him. Thinking about it all later, ours resembled a "friendly uncle, curious teenage niece" relationship. I enjoyed my newfound stature as his bride, and resented it when his colleagues referred to me teasingly as Walter's "child bride."

Walter took me to the physician's bowling club, and I took to the sport immediately. Soon I vied successfully with some of their better bowlers, but Walter showed little pleasure when we all kidded him about his clumsy attempts at bowling. We soon stopped this form of recreation.

When I was back in Berlin, much was discussed about the furniture my parents planned to send to Gmünd for my future apartment there. And Mother let me decide which of the family china sets, silverware, bed and table linens, and knick-knacks I desired. My parents were always of the opinion that children should get their inheritance when they needed it, and not just when their parents died. Mother also bought furniture cheaply for me from some members of the parish. And finally the truck was on its way to Gmünd, where Walter would take over.

Time flew by with all these preparations and with my strenuous hospital job. It was the end of March now, and the wedding gown was being designed by Odi. She and Helmut were engaged now, but were not planning to marry until fall. She did not mind that I was going to beat her to the altar, but that victory over my older sister was still very important to me.

Dreams Must Dissipate
April 1943 to June 1943

It was the middle of April in 1943, with just one and a half months to go 'til the wedding. I was on my way home from the day shift at the hospital, clad in my nurse's uniform and wearily hanging on to the strap of the overcrowded subway. As I glanced around, my eyes rested momentarily on a quietly conversing, handsome couple by the opposite door. She was a beautiful woman, dressed expensively but tastefully, while he was "tall, dark, and handsome." His major's uniform fit him to perfection. He looked so elegant and "man of the world" that my mind wistfully compared him to Walter for a moment. I looked away, but his eyes caught my glance. Their door opened and they were gone. I forgot them.

A week later one of my co-students suggested that we should spend our belated lunch hour at the noted sidewalk café Kranzler. We walked across the "Ku-Damm" and entered the café itself, rather than sitting outside, because we had left without our coats. We were led to a table near the grand piano and ordered tea and a piece of their delicious pastry, for which I had saved up on my ration card, just in case.

Later, as we smoked and talked, a waiter rolled up a serving table to us. It held an ice bucket with a bottle of champagne, two long-stemmed glasses, and one even longer-stemmed rosebud. The waiter asked me if I would accept this from a "gentleman," and he discretely nodded toward a table across the aisle on the other side of the piano. Three officers were seated there. One of them arose briefly now, smiled and saluted. It was the "subway major"! I felt myself blushing as my girlfriend enjoyed herself hugely over my embarrassment. She gurgled, "Oh, he's gorgeous!" I laughed and nodded our thanks slightly in his direction. As we enjoyed the champagne he came to our table and introduced himself. My friend suddenly decided that she had to get back to the hospital. And now I found myself actually sitting in the Kranzler with a "dreamboat," who looked more handsome and distinguished than any of my movie idols! Suddenly, this Berlin, which I had hated for so many years, became paradise.

Stunned and flattered that he had remembered me from that fleeting glance, I tried to ask him as casually as possible about the lovely woman who had been his companion. I was amazed about myself that I dared to bring up the subject but the champagne had loosened my tongue, and his answer would determine my further conduct. He laughed and said that he did not want to use the old "cousin" routine, but that she had been his date at times, and that they had parted amicably forever.

My fiancé, the upcoming wedding, and my parents were forgotten! All I could feel was an overwhelming desire to know this man and to make him forget "her" completely. He escorted me back to the hospital, and we made a date for the following evening—a Friday—at a small, exclusive Hungarian restaurant.

Although much of that night I felt badly about Walter and our families, I did not really feel guilty. I was determined to finally have a chance to follow my heart, rather than my brain. And needing to find out, once and for all, what passion was all about, while ordering myself not to worry about consequences!

My parents believed that I was going to dine out with girlfriends right after work, and that we would see a show, also. I took my best dress with me to the hospital, as well as my only high-heeled shoes, make-up and cigarettes, of course, and Walter's Paris perfume.

I met him at about 6:00 PM at the restaurant, where he was waiting for me. He kissed my hand and led me to one of the secluded tables. I loved the décor of wine-red and gold, the sole lighting being candles, and huge vases of fresh flowers everywhere. A native-clad Hungarian band of mainly violins played a *czardas*, the gypsy-type rhythm I loved, with the violins wailing about the loneliness of the endless *puszta*.

He was obviously known there, and we were waited on to perfection. When the orchestra changed to dance tunes we got up and his dancing was as perfect as everything else about him. I closed my eyes and he led our bodies to complete harmony. Everything I had dreamed about for years came together in this one man and this one moment.

We ate the delicious Hungarian goulash (his ration allotment was far more generous than mine), and we talked and danced and talked some more. And then he sat suddenly by my side on the little settee, and I was in his arms as we kissed... A trio of violin-playing Hungarians standing by our side and serenading us brought us back to reality, and we hummed the lovely tunes and he paid them well.

The place closed early, as all restaurants did because of the possibility of air raids. We walked in the middle of the dark and quiet street, still humming. Then we started to dance. We danced half the night in that little street. And in between we kissed and kissed.

He had totally swept me off my feet. The next few weeks were heaven on earth as we met at every opportunity. He was an Austrian career officer on a three-month assignment in Berlin. His family was wealthy, owning a string of hotels in Vienna and Salzburg. I loved the pictures of his childhood, his family, his dogs, and his beloved Austrian Alps. We always met on neutral ground. He had no idea where I lived, and I did not ask his address, either. He had noticed my engagement ring, of course, but I dodged his question and I let neither one of us think much about anything but our love affair.

Never again in my later life was I this passionately kissed, caressed, spoiled, and celebrated by any man. He even stayed by my first floor hospital window when I was on night duty. He watched me as I took care of the babies, and he waited patiently for me. Whenever I had a short break I sneaked out to him through a seldom-used side door, for which I had wrangled a key. Outside it was pitch-dark in a little garden, except on the nights when the searchlights from the three flak towers skimmed the skies looking for the advancing planes. When the sirens sounded

I helped to transfer the babies to the cellar, but then I went out through "our" door, where he was waiting. And he kissed me and caressed me even while the bombs fell not too far from us. We both knew that a direct hit would penetrate any cellar anyway, and that our chances of survival were not much worse on the street, rather than being buried in the rubble of any building. Besides, death had been my shadow for so much of my youth that I refused to let it darken the sun for me now.

I knew that he wanted more from me than I was willing to give. I had recently pestered my sister to explain sex to me, and she had done so, especially since Mother had asked her to "illuminate me" before the wedding. When he realized now that, despite my eagerness to please him I was not ready to give myself totally to him, he asked me to marry him.

I truly had not thought much about that possibility. From the outset he had seemed to me much too gorgeous and much too charming to picture him with any one woman for any length of time. To this day I believe that even if I had not been engaged to another man I would not have married him. Just thinking about marriage made my brain take over for my emotion, and it told me clearly that I did not wish to marry any man who would probably not be faithful to me in the long run.

I explained to him now that I would be married soon to a much less gorgeous but much more reliable man. I also described my role as an obedient clergyman's daughter, and my dread to upset both families and to disappoint the entire parish, which was waiting eagerly to watch my wedding.

He was, of course, horrified that I would marry someone out of fear to enrage or disappoint others. He admitted that he had been something of a Lothario—especially as compared to my fiancé—but he assured me urgently that he would love me forever and that he would change. I had to laugh and told him that he reminded me of a beautiful leopard who could not, and never should, change his spots. I did not tell him my most important reason for refusing him, namely that we were much too much alike! I was as impulsive, generous, and as ready for adventure as he was and needed a man who would have a stabilizing influence on my own, sometimes self-destructive, nature.

At our last date, exactly a week before the wedding, he threatened half-kiddingly, half-seriously, that he would find me in the church and drag me away from the altar, shouting to all that I really loved him and not Walter. Then he would take me with him to his beloved Alps, where we would live happily ever after. I kissed him through my tears, and I turned and left him.

Now I threw myself with body, but not soul, into the last-minute preparations for the big event. Not daring to think much, I just wanted to get it over with now.

We all prayed for relatively bomb-free nights. We were jubilant that the Allies had defeated the Axis in Africa. Surrender to us meant countless lives saved, and the end of the Reich coming closer.

For June fourth, the day before the wedding, hotel reservations had been made for Walter and 20 of his relatives and friends. They were resting up now for the evening, which in Germany is called *Polterabend* ("clatter evening"). That is a pre-nuptial party, where, at midnight, old, inexpensive crockery and china is smashed and swept up by the bride and groom. The symbolism escapes me, but I looked forward to the fun.

We had chosen the yacht club for the event, and after inspecting our boat—where Walter and I were left "tactfully" alone for a while—the guests assembled in the large, festively decorated clubhouse hall, complete with bar and a band.

The evening was a perfect success. We had invited about 70 guests, and—at Odi's, Hans's and my insistence—half of the guests were young people. I remember dancing with all of them, and some of the older folks to boot. I exhilarated in my last hours of "singledom" and was touched by so much outpouring of love for me. Father had worked hard, and finally successfully, on Hans's flak tower commander to let him have the evening off. As Hans and I danced now he said suddenly, "I know you don't love him. And I sense why you are doing this. Are you sure that an unhappy marriage will set you free? Remember, you and I have run away before. If you want to escape now I will help you. You know I will!" I smiled up at him, "Hans, as long as I have you, nothing terrible will ever happen to me. Let me try this. I need this change from home. I will call out to you if I'm in trouble." He then asked, "Promise?" I pressed his hand and nodded, before others cut in to dance with me.

Gifts and speeches, embraces and tears. And at midnight glass and china was smashed with abundance on the front porch, where Walter and I tried to sweep up the mess rather unsuccessfully.

The wedding was set for 3:00 PM the next day. At 11:00 AM I found myself with Walter at the marriage bureau located at the Alexander Platz. There the state married us officially. Church weddings did not legalize a marriage then. To us, of course, this was just a dumb formality.

Out of Step

Father had rejected as silly the custom of the bride and groom arriving at the church in a black, shiny, rented carriage drawn by four white horses. Instead, we all paraded by foot from the Heim to the church. Hundreds of parishioners and neighbors lined the sidewalks and cheered and clapped as we walked by. I waved back and smiled—I had not disappointed them.

Two little flower girls led us, followed by Walter and me, with my veil being carried by two little boys. Then came Father with Walter's father, both clergymen wearing their most formal Lutheran robes and berets. They were followed by Walter's mother and mine. Both ladies were wearing black-lace evening gowns and each carried a bouquet of white narcissis. Odi, on Helmut's arm, was next. And then grandmother followed on the arm of her granddaughter from Kassel. Walter's brothers were absent. All invited guests now followed in twos.

Hans was not with us. I was never sure if he had not been permitted to take the day off, or if he would not have any part in this…

I will skip the lengthy ceremony here, but I tried valiantly to get in the mood, and I honestly promised to "honor and obey" as both fathers took turns in performing the ritual. Our church was full to overflowing, and outside throngs were waiting to line more sidewalks as our parade now wound itself from the church to our Samariter haus and to our apartment.

All was in readiness at home for about 60 dinner guests. The tables stretched from the salon through the waiting room and into Father's study. Aunt Oda, who was present, and had helped with cooking, had brought chickens, pork, and baking ingredients from Beyersdorf (in spite of strict government laws forbidding this). My sister had baked the wedding cake. Grandmother had tried to be helpful by baking sheets and sheets of *kuchen* for the parishioners who would be appearing at the door to congratulate. But Grandmother's tastebuds had dulled to the point where she could not tell salt from sugar. Everything had to be baked anew just before the ceremony. But generally, all went smoothly.

One of my most treasured presents was a home-bound book of poems Father had made, describing with great humor and wit my "characteristic" deeds, events and happenings from my birth to the present. Odi had illustrated each poem cleverly to make it funny. Our Stuttgart guests ate and drank to their hearts' content, and toasted the happy couple. They were very impressed with our beautiful china, but I was taken aback when I overheard "Mama" pointing out to "Papa" that all this Meissen and Bavarian china would be sent to Gmünd after the wedding and would belong to their family from now on. I winced and swore silently to myself that no matter whom I married, Harnisch things would remain Harnisch things!

The doorbell rang almost uninterruptedly, with well-wishers and gifts and telegrams and flowers. One was a huge floral display. It took two men to bring it upstairs, and on the stand were fastened roses and roses and roses. There was no card. Everyone assumed that the florist had forgotten to attach it, but Odi looked at me quizzically. I thanked the major silently for having been by my side from afar and having understood.

The tables were moved out of the way and someone started to play dance music on "Gisela's piano" (my grand piano had been shipped to Gmünd, together with my furniture). I was all set to dance again when Odi and Mother appeared at my elbow and whispered it was "time." I glanced at Walter and he looked exasperated already. I sighed and retired to my room, where my suit had been laid out. While I changed I looked once more at the wardrobes of zoo and hot chocolate fame, at the laundry hamper with Berthold, and at my bed and desk. And then the waiting cab whisked Walter and me away.

When we were alone in the hotel room, he took me in his arms and kissed me. But these were still "brother-sister" kisses! I was totally confused now. Was he naïve? But he was ten years older than I; he had to know by now. Was he just careful according to parental instructions? Was he too shy? Maybe I needed to take the initiative. I did. He stepped back as if stung by a wasp. And to my utter amazement and fury I was told that "only loose women kiss like that." I was French kissing, and how would I possibly know this unless I was a lot less innocent than I and my parents had made him believe.

My first reaction was to slap his face and to leave. But I controlled myself and assured him that I was not a bad girl, but that he was about 100 years behind the times. Every girl, whether good or bad, kissed like that nowadays. But if he did not like it I would not do it again.

We went to bed, each on our own side. I pretended to be bone-tired as he now began to talk into the darkness about not having to worry about sex yet because he fully agreed with my parents that I was too young, and that he was willing to wait a while. I did not answer, and he was quiet then.

The next afternoon we took the night train to Munich. No sleeper compartments were available, since all of those had been turned over to the military. Every compartment was packed. But at least we had found seats.

Now Walter told me where we were headed. He had made all the reservations, and I was to be surprised. We would spend three days in Munich, one week in a lovely Austrian mountain village, and finally four more days in Salzburg, the Mozart city.

Although I personally would have preferred Vienna, I assured him that he had planned a fine trip. Then we had dinner in the elegant dining car. It was crammed also, and the food was skimpy, despite our ration cards. With horror I then watched as he carefully counted out nickels and dimes for the waiter's tip. Oh god, what else would I have to discover about my husband? Maybe I was always too generous, but a stingy man? I quickly added to the tip as the waiter picked up Walter's coins and I pretended to be unaware of my husband paling and biting his lip.

Matters got worse. I had discovered at the hotel that Mother had stuffed one of my two suitcases with a huge, hard salami (from Aunt Oda) and many other goodies. I was still hungry and unpacked some of these provisions. Then I realized that everyone hungrily watched Walter and I eat. I could not stand that and began to share my food with everyone. Walter tried to stop me, and when that failed he angrily left the compartment. That was fine with me, and after eating we began to sing and talk and play parlor games deep into the night. I had no idea where my husband was, and I frankly couldn't care less.

Munich was lovely. But I soon found out that with Walter every museum and church had to be compulsively seen inside and out, regardless of time pressure or the blisters on one's feet. I finally left him to explore further on his own, while I sat in a library or a picture gallery or a sidewalk café until he met me again.

I think it was on the second day of our stay in Munich, while walking across a bridge, that Walter accidentally spilled some pennies down to the embankment below. To my amazement and embarrassment, my fully uniformed husband climbed from the bridge down onto the embankment. There he searched carefully for every missing penny. Passersby were beginning to congregate on the bridge. They obviously thought that he was looking for something valuable. I had enough, and took the next streetcar back to the hotel. I was aware that I had wanted a husband who was somewhat less generous than I was, but this was far more difference than I had wanted or hoped for. I took a nap and refused to answer when he finally came in after looking all over the city for me.

Then came the Austrian Alps. They were every bit as beautiful as "my major" had described them to me. We stayed at a picturesque hotel in a lovely little village that was off the beaten path—at least in the summer time. It was mainly a ski resort, complete with ski tows, and it was devoid of tourists in the summer. I soon realized why. All the winter snow that made the place famous came down as summer rain and fog. As far as I remember, we had exactly one sunny day during that week.

I suppose one could have made the best of it by concentrating on indoor activities such as Ping-pong or reading. Or one could have taken day trips to better climes. But to my husband, mountains were made for climbing. Period. Need I say much more? We spent day after day slipping, sliding and crawling up and down the mountains. We got lost several times because I had paid no attention, and Walter had absolutely no sense of direction. My clothes were soaked, my shoes ruined, my hairdo unrecognizable, and my feet covered with blisters. After three days of this nightmare I went on strike and let him crawl around the dripping mountains all by himself.

But the worst times were the nights. I was still hoping for some kind of romance to be budding. I knew he was tempted and I wore less and less clothing around the room. Then, one night, he finally tried it. But it was hopelessly futile. Was he that inexperienced? Was he sick? Was he gay? I jumped up and went out on to the balcony, staring hopelessly into the night and fog.

After a while I went to the desk and turned on the little lamp. Then I wrote to Odi, with page after page featuring my despair. I even told her about "my major," and how I wished now that I had given in to his pleading and had sex with him, so that I would have been happy and fulfilled at least once in my life, even if I would not have married him.

I was so engrossed that I did not realize right away that my husband had gotten up and was standing behind me, reading every word I was writing. When I became aware of him, I hesitated for just a moment but then continued my tale about my "miserable" marriage. I knew full well that I was being very cruel. In fact, I had never realized that I was capable of such cruelty. But I could not help myself anymore. After I sealed the letter I asked my husband to please mail it on his way to the mountains. Then I went to bed and to sleep.

He did mail that letter to Odi and for the next couple of days his manner was a lot less arrogant, overbearing and lecturing. On the only sunny day I climbed with him all the way up to the ski tow. The hotel up there was closed for the summer, but the view was spectacular. We picnicked on the way down and Walter painted me under a pine tree with the red and white tablecloth by my side.

Salzburg found us both in a forgiving mood. The city was so entrancingly beautiful and sunny that I kept pace with my husband as we visited the many castles and churches. At night we sat in an outdoor amphitheater and enjoyed the orchestra playing Mozart's lovely music. I finally succumbed to Austria's charm.

Yet the ever-present Nazi uniforms, and the fervent "Heil Hitler" with which every waiter, waitress, and hotel clerk greeted us, was beginning to get on my nerves. It was time to leave.

You're On Your Own

July 1943 to April 1944

Schwäbisch-Gmünd, the charming medieval little town in South Germany which I had already scouted in March, became my home. We locals called it Gmünd for short, for the full name was too cumbersome even for German tongues.

My parents had sent a truckload of furniture, linen, china, and books to our first floor, two-room apartment in the stately Lutheran manse on the hill overlooking the town. My husband continued his work as a staff physician at the local military and civilian hospital downtown. He had a room there and an office and was served three meals daily. Even though he was a general physician he had to do a lot of surgery on the wounded, under the supervision of the chief surgeon, who was not very impressed with his surgical skills.

I proceeded now happily to furnish and decorate my first and own apartment. Because furniture was not available in stores any more, Mother had bought a bedroom suite for me cheaply from an elderly couple who, like thousands of other Berliners, had fled to the safer countryside. So one of my two large, bright rooms—which had formerly been offices—became now a comfortable bedroom, with a large picture window facing the town below.

Adjoining the bedroom was the living-dining room, complete with my parents' large china cabinet and matching table and chairs. Across the room stood the small grey-striped couch and two little matching easy chairs encircling a round, glass-top coffee table. My in-laws had sent a lady's rolltop desk and a glass door bookcase from Stuttgart, which completed the room. Here, too, was a picture window, but this one faced the rear garden and the wooded hillside.

In both rooms the windows were partially shrouded with billowing white curtains, but the inevitable blackout shades had to be drawn down and tightly shut at night. The floors were beautifully kept inlaid parquet, and both rooms had a small iron pot-bellied stove. But even when I was able to get some coal or wood they never really managed to warm the rooms sufficiently.

Because this first floor of the manse had been designed for offices only I had neither a kitchen nor a bath. A small, unheated toilet featured the only running water, but it was cold. The toilet had no flusher at all, so one used a pitcher.

The also unheated, stone-floored entrance hall became my kitchen. At least it was very large and able to accommodate my grand piano, which Mother had sent to me despite my protestations. Well, at any rate no one was here to force me to play it. Stoves could not be bought either. After a desperate search I located a small two-burner unit, which I placed on a chair. It used coal or wood, and it took forever just to boil a pot of cold water drawn from the restroom. For dishwashing I filled a pan with the water and a tiny amount of soap allotted on my ration card. This was my kitchen—period. Refrigerators were not even known then in Germany, and I bicycled twice a week to the downtown market and shops for groceries.

But if one ignored the primitive utilities one could still enjoy the two nice rooms, which became my private haven.

Allied bombers flew in groups almost nightly—and soon days, too—at great heights above our town. But their deadly loads were meant for cities farther east, such as Dresden and Munich. Although the sirens wailed frequently, one felt fairly secure in this small town, with the roofs of the three hospitals clearly marked with red crosses. The second hospital in Gmünd was a children's hospital, and the third one was for tuberculosis only, located quite isolated on the opposite hillside.

Only when Stuttgart got bombed about 50 miles west of Gmünd did we hear the explosions like distant thunder, and the windows rattled. Then I cowered in the moldy cellar, together with the clergy couple from upstairs and their two teenaged children. The wife, being of British origin, could have left Germany years ago. But she preferred to stay with her family. They also had fled Berlin.

I did not have much time to get settled. This was the summer of 1943, and even though Hitler deployed millions of forced laborers from Nazi-occupied countries, there was still a shortage of arms production workers, farmers, nurses, teachers and many professionals. Unless one had a medical excuse one had to work, otherwise the ration card would not be allotted.

I was not about to help Hitler with his insane war by working in an arms factory. So I talked my husband into pressuring the pediatric hospital, which was located at the outskirts of town, to accept me as a student nurse. They did take me, but it was not a simple matter. The hospital was a Catholic facility and staffed only by nuns. All their student nurses were asked to become full-fledged nuns at the end of their three-year training period. The only other kind of student nurses there were paid girls from the Nazi party in emblem-marked uniforms, whose leader was a fanatic old maid who adored the Führer. The hospital had been forced to accept them. I did, of course, not belong to either group, and with my Berlin uniforms and cap I stuck out like a sore thumb. My being a north German did not sit well either because of the centuries-old rivalry between north and south. Although I was used to being "different" from childhood on, I had no family here to back me up.

My husband and I saw little of each other. He had frequently night duty, and my work schedule, which averaged 12 hours a day, was also irregular. When we happened to have the same day off we hiked to the nearby mountains and picked wildflowers and berries, or sold some silverware to remotely-situated farmers for a piece of ham or a bit of butter. I was often so exhausted from my nursing duties that I would have preferred to stay at home. The lack of good food began to weaken my health, too. Although my husband brought me occasionally some leftover hospital food, there was still a constant lack of meat, fish, dairy foods, eggs, and fats.

One rainy Sunday in July I woke up with urinary frequency and pain. Walter gave me some sulfur pills, and still insisted on a walk. The pain became more agonizing with every mile we hiked. I urinated constantly behind bushes and trees. By the time we finally reached home I had a raging fever and was taken to the hospital by ambulance.

My husband showed not the slightest remorse when he made his twice-daily rounds to my room, accompanied by the efficient nuns. I was given antibiotics, intravenous fluids and painkillers, and eventually the excruciating pain subsided. The diagnosis revealed that the urinary infection had reached my right kidney, and for many years to come that kidney tended to infect and the area was badly scarred.

Rather weak yet I nevertheless returned to work, and was promptly assigned to the contagious ward. There, two of my little patients had diphtheria, and despite all precautions I came down with it. Back to the downtown hospital I went, this time into a quarantined room with no visitors allowed. I had not realized before that a throat could hurt this much, and the fever left me delirious and barely conscious. When I finally recovered I had to spend another week in that room. The window faced the courtyard, and I watched the many recuperating and often badly maimed soldiers resting or playing games out there, or eating their lunch. Finally I was allowed some fresh air and exercise, too, and I joined the men outside. We played games and laughed and sang together and I quickly became the life of the party. My husband found my behavior undignified and certainly not befitting a physician's wife. But I ignored him and was happy.

The little town had several goldsmith shops where the owners were artists who still handcrafted their gorgeous jewelry. Many of them had also designed and produced the altars and Madonna statues in the various churches and cathedrals in the entire south German area. I was allowed to have a lovely, medieval design, gold and jewel ring, completely handcrafted. It even featured my family's coat of arms. Walter, too, had one made for himself, with his family seal on it which could be used on hot wax for sealing.

There was also an artist colony in Gmünd with young and old painters and sculptors, musicians and dancers. Most of them were refugees, too, and they welcomed me despite my total lack of artistic talents. I felt easy and free in their warm and liberal company. One famous sculptor and professional was a "native," and had a villa and a huge atelier on my hillside. There he created massive bigger-than-life statues and other sculptures, with the help of the most talented of his art students. He asked my husband's permission to sculpt my head, for he loved my face and was eager to try it. And so I spent many of my scarce free hours for the next two months modeling. We did pay him a commission, but much below the price he usually asked for his work.

It was fascinating to watch him mold my head in clay, first in small and then in ever larger sizes. The final product was somewhat bigger than my own head. He complained how difficult it was to get the eyes just right, because "your eyes are so expressive and so alive. That makes it hard to do them justice in clay and plaster." When the weather was nice he worked outdoors, with flowerbeds and butterflies all around us. We talked of many things. He was

My head as sculpted in 1943

anti-Nazi, yet to my chagrin he had accepted several orders for statues from such monsters as Hitler's field marshal Hermann Göring. But I suppose his life would have been in danger had he refused to accept these assignments.

The highlight of that August was for me a two-day visit from my brother Hans, my sister Odi, and her fiancé Helmut Bott from Berlin. Hans, now 16, had been drafted into the cavalry and was training at a military camp near Berlin. He managed to get a short furlough at the same time Helmut was also in Berlin on a furlough from the Russian front.

Walter and I reserved rooms for them at the old Royal Inn by the marketplace downtown, and we both managed to get two days off from our respective hospitals. Now the five of us explored the old town. My sister, who by now was majoring in art and architecture, explained much to us about the history and styles of the various churches and the cathedral from ancient Romanic, to Gothic, to Baroque. I proudly showed them my apartment, and we even visited my children's hospital where I had made friends with several nursing students.

We talked until deep into the nights. On the second day Hans, Odi and I sang our beloved old folk songs as we walked on shaded paths in a little park on the outskirts of Gmünd. And we dangled our legs from an old pier into the little frog pond there—a short respite from the horrors of the outside world. Much of our discussions centered around Odi and Helmut's wedding plans for October in Berlin, which I hoped to be able to attend.

I accompanied them back on the local train from Gmünd to Stuttgart, from where the three then continued on northward to Berlin on an express train. We hugged and cried when we parted, because in these times every good-bye could be the last one.

During July and August of 1943, despite all Nazi propaganda, the war had reached the turning point. Rumors had it that after a successful tank battle the Russian army was slowly pushing the German army back. On July 10 the Allies had invaded Sicily under the command of General Patton. And the United States and British navies had become powerful enough by now to sink German U-boats faster than they could be replaced. So the Atlantic was safe for the Allies.

Walter's wound had sufficiently healed, and he received his travel orders to a field hospital in Russia. Our marriage had been merely a living arrangement, but now I dreaded the prospect of being totally alone. I cried when he boarded the crowded troop train, and, could see hope in his eyes that I might grow to love him after all. But I knew that my pain was purely selfish, and I felt guilty about my emptiness.

Walter's parents had fled from the increasing air attacks on Stuttgart to a village about one-third down the highway toward Gmünd. My father-in-law became rector of the ancient village church, and they lived quite comfortably at the rectory. Their loyal live-in maid also moved with them. Surrounded by farms and vineyards they were fairly well provided with food from their parishioners. We all were much too busy to visit each other, but they called me at times. Their youngest son, Fritz, had been seriously wounded on the western front. I visited him at a veteran's hospital near Ulm. He was in great pain, and he had aged so much beyond his 23 years. The expression in his eyes was absent and haunted. He had seen and experienced unspeakable horrors at the front, which he could not relate in any detail.

My job at the children's hospital was in some respects a blessing. It kept me too busy and tired to feel lonely. Some excellent local physicians and pediatricians gave lectures almost daily, and so did some of the nuns. I was allowed to help with baby deliveries in the maternity ward, feeling much sympathy for mothers who had to bring babies into this world of war and hunger and hate.

The pediatric hospital where Gisela trained as a nurse. (Photo taken in 1994.)

Among the Catholic student nurses I found a few who shared my political views. We became thick friends, and because most of them lived in the hospital's dreary dorms they loved spending some evenings at my apartment. There we could talk without fear of spies listening, and we munched on some precious deserts from their hospital meals. One of them confided in me that she was in love with a French prisoner of war, who was assigned at times to help at her parent's farm. They were planning on fleeing to France, but I implored her to remain safely here until Germany would be hopefully defeated.

Once a week in the hospital auditorium all staff members were forced to listen to a lecture by a powerful Nazi *Gauleiter*. He was the town's principle political "supervisor." In other words, he was the head of a Nazi spy network that was always looking for "traitors" to arrest. Such men operated in every city and all villages throughout Germany.

Even senior nuns and the two priests were forced to attend this man's propaganda and hate speeches. Being an "outsider" no one had ordered me to attend, so I stayed away. But my friends told me some of the man's outrageous lies and ravings against Jews, Gypsies, and even priests. My fury overcame all caution, and I decided to attend a lecture. After he had opened with praise for the party, the troops, and the war heroes, he launched into a hate tirade against intellectuals. From there he went on to attack Lutheran resistance clergy, like Dr. Martin Niemöller, as being traitors. When he claimed that there were "4,000 such clergy and vicars undermining the will of the German people to fight the enemies of the Reich" I raised my hand. He smiled and asked me to speak. I rose and addressed the audience, rather than him, with something like this: "I beg to differ here. Much of the resistance movement within the Lutheran Church is a matter of Christian conscience, which is at times at odds with Nazi doctrines. And being the daughter of such a clergyman I happen to know that there are not even close to 4,000 clergy and vicars in all of Germany, and much less among the resistance clergy. The number is about 1,500. It seems that a speaker of such political stature as this gentleman should be better informed before he accuses." With that I left the auditorium, with my steps dramatically audible in the stunned silence.

I must admit that I was shaking inside. People had been whisked away to prisons for openly defying these powerful and ruthless Nazis. I sweated a few nights waiting to be arrested, but perhaps because there had been so many witnesses I got away with my protest.

To my amazement I became something like a heroine to most of the hospital's staff. The nuns had mainly ignored me before, but this changed drastically. Smiles and kisses greeted me daily, and I was even invited to share breakfast with them. They fed me fresh rolls and hot chocolate, which I had not tasted in years. My friends adored me, and I heard that more and more people now stood up and argued with the Nazi during his lectures. The only person who hated me more than ever was the Nazi head nurse. But I was able to ignore her rude remarks, because my care for the sick children was untiring and conscientious. She could find no reason to have me expelled.

I must add one note here to the entire episode. I did not have the foggiest idea how many Lutheran clergymen there existed in Germany. But I had figured rightly that he did not know, either...

The bad habit of staying up late nights and being dead-tired mornings had me in its grip again. Luckily, one of my friends by the name of Hedwig lived just downhill from me. She rang my bell every morning, and if I had overslept she helped me to race out of the house, and then we bicycled together to the hospital. Her parents were secretly anti-Nazi, too, and as gentle and kind as she was. Her father had been mayor of Gmünd many years ago, but had been replaced by a Nazi puppet.

Walter wrote frequently. He had caught scarlet fever soon after arriving in Russia and was recuperating in a hospital in Poland. His letters consisted mainly of poetic descriptions of the countryside and old cemeteries and such. It was enviable how this man could shut out reality—especially since this escapism released one from responsibility. How angry he would have been, for instance, had he known about my little speech at the hospital, but eventually he would have written poems about it all...

When October came I was ready for my trip to Berlin. Train travel was beginning to be risky because of occasional air attacks on stations. But I was lucky.

Odi's and Helmut's wedding was much simpler than mine had been, since survival was more on everyone's mind than festivities. Food was getting scarcer by the week. The gasoline shortage alone made it difficult for transports from the countryside to reach the millions of hungry Berliners.

Odi and Helmut were much in love. They were a beautiful couple. Like all other young lovers they had so little time together before the men had to get back to the front. Our former playroom had been turned into a living room for them, and my own former room had become their bedroom.

Grandmother was there, too. She was 80 years old and well, despite her diminutive and frail frame. Hans had only one day off, and each hour with him was precious.

Father and Mother looked pale and tired, but they continued to help their parishioners, especially the old and infirm. There was no nursing home in the district, so my parents had turned the large parish hall downstairs into a shelter for lonely and ailing elderly parishioners. The hall accommodated about 40 beds, and the small kitchen facility produced three meals daily with the help of volunteers.

Father's shelter for the aged and sick in East Berlin. After 1945 it was used to shelter girls at night to keep them safe from getting raped by Russian soldiers.

The resistance (BK) churches of Berlin collected funds to pay for a registered nurse and a physiotherapist.

I caught up on the latest parish news about the dead, missing and wounded among our friends and acquaintances. Even Berthold, Hans's and my little childhood friend, had been sent to the eastern front and had not been heard from since. His parents were already mourning the death of Berthold's older brother, Günther. Uncle Alexander's oldest boy, Uli, had also been killed. And three of Father's former assistant clergymen had been drafted, with two of them already dead. And the carnage went on...

So far our district of Berlin was not badly bombed, and except for some damage to the roof by small firebombs, the church was also still standing tall.

Dr. Martin Niemöller, the brave spokesman for the BK resistance, had been arrested. Rumor had it that he had been taken to the concentration camp Sachsenhausen. We feared for his life and the lives of many others in captivity. All we could do for them was pray.

My few days in Berlin seemed to fly, and then I was back in Gmünd, and alone.

With few exceptions, Germans were still fanatically believing in Hitler and his final victory, which would then be followed by German domination over the whole world. They truly felt they were a chosen people and superior to all other nations and races. Propaganda Minister Joseph Göbbel's machine kept these insane beliefs alive in the people, despite their cities being bombed, their hunger becoming more gnawing, and their soldiers coming home on furloughs with whispered stories of losing battles and countless fatalities. By now, the draft age had become ever younger and ever older, the food lines ever longer, the Allied bombing ever more precise. The blame for all this was simply laid on the world's Jews, the inferior foreign nations who had always hated Germany, on the Treaty of Versailles, and on whatever. After all, Germany was just defending itself against it's sworn enemies, and the Third Reich would definitely prevail for all eternity!

At night I pressed my ear close to the radio, trying to catch bits of actual world news from such stations as Basel in Switzerland, which sometimes could be heard over the static. I discerned that Italy had probably secretly surrendered in September already, but that German troops there fought the Allies every step since they had landed in Salerno. There were especially bloody battles in the area around Cassino.

I dreaded the winter like everyone else did. My coal ration was so small that I could see my breath in the two heated rooms. And many a morning I found every drop of water frozen in the toilet and in the kitchen. When the snows came down, Hedwig and I sledded downhill to get to the hospital in the morning.

Walter had been sent to a field hospital now, which was usually located directly behind the front line. From the reports of recovering soldiers downtown, we all knew that the entire eastern armies were bogged down in snow and ice. Walter's brother Fritz, barely recovered, had been sent back to the western front. Father's brother, my Uncle Siegfried, supervised rebuilding of blown-up bridges in Belgium. The oldest of his two boys, Friedrich Wilhelm, had been drafted now at age 14. And Uncle Engbert, Mother's brother, was again forced into a uniform, even though he had already served in WWI. He was currently stationed in Yugoslavia, where he had to repair electricity works.

One Sunday night I was awakened by a light, but persistent knocking on the front door. A German soldier asked me to let him in because he had some important matters to discuss with me. He identified himself as a member of a German underground network. I did not ask him why he trusted me, and I didn't ask his name, either. I just let him in and listened.

He brought a bundle of leaflets with him, printed in England. They told of German defeats and warned of terrible air raids to come. They asked the German people to lay down their arms, to refuse to fight, and to help bring down the horrible regime of Adolf Hitler.

The man gave me no instructions what to do with the leaflets. He simply gave them to me after I had read one. Then he left. I hid them for a few days while I waited to see if this was a trap and if I would be watched. But no one seemed to trail me, and slowly an idea formed in my mind what to do.

On a moonless evening I took the last evening train to a town called Aalen, which lay about 10 miles east of Gmünd. Aalen was a crossing point for trains from several directions. I waited near the station, and when all was deserted and quiet I set out across the rails to several commuter trains, which were standing dark and silent on sidings and in the rail yard. As I had scouted beforehand, these trains would be moving and filling with commuters by morning.

The doors were not locked, to my relief, and with a pounding heart I scurried through several trains and their compartments, laying the leaflets on the seats. I dared not take a hotel in town, but spent the rest of the night and part of the morning on a park bench, shaking with cold, tiredness, and fear. Then I took a train back to Gmünd.

My knees were still weak for a few days, and I hoped I would never be contacted again for a task like this one. But eventually I was simply proud and happy that I had been able to help a little with making a difference.

Mother wrote that Pastor Dr. Niemöller had been transferred to the concentration camp Dachau. His wife had heard it, along with information that he was starving. Over time, I sent several packages of food to him, but was never sure if he ever received them.

When the spring of 1944 finally came, the fighting on all fronts increased again. Walter's brother Fritz was killed now, and so was Uncle Siegfried, Father's brother. I often wondered if he finally realized that Father had been right when they had argued about the topic of military obedience years ago. Had the man finally admitted to himself that this was not a "war of defense," and that no one could remain an "honorable career officer" under a power hungry dictatorship?

As more of my fellow student nurses graduated, many of them left, most often to their hometowns. The workload became overwhelming and depressing. But at least the days and nights grew warmer.

In March, my father-in-law called me with the news that Walter would arrive shortly in Stuttgart for a few days furlough. I took a week off from work and went by train to Stuttgart. I was glad to see him. He looked tired but well. He had been promoted by two ranks, so he had the medical rank equivalent to a major now. His salary had been raised accordingly, but money had become almost useless because food and all necessities of life had become very scarce or totally nonexistent. Black market trading of goods was now punishable by imprisonment or even death.

We spent the night in Stuttgart because it was late and the trains had stopped running. His parents had kept their apartment in the city, but in the meantime half of that high-rise building had been bombed right down the middle into rubble. So both bedrooms, the study, both balconies and one quarter of the kitchen had been razed. To keep the weather out, sheets of black plastic covered the gaping sides, where one false step would send one three stories down into the heap of concrete rubble. The only still remaining areas were the staircase, the living room and the music room. The latter had a bed in it, in case family members of friends needed temporary shelter. There was no electricity nor water, of course.

We spent the night in the music room, and we had intercourse. I felt no passion, just the need to be close to someone. I had been alone with my fears for a long time.

After a few days in Gmünd he left me again on a troop train. And again I cried.

After he was gone, I began to chafe more and more at my long hours at the hospital. I knew full well that Walter wanted me to get the nursing degree, but it was dubious if I would receive it since I was not registered with either student contingent.

To find another job turned out to be much easier than I had thought. A combination Kindergarten-nursery school was located just downhill from me, where my street curved into the town. It was also a Catholic facility, run single-handedly by a tall, middle-aged, friendly nun. When I asked her if she could use me as an assistant she hired me on the spot. Her last assistant had just left, and she had "heard good things" about me. So I began my new career.

There were about 20 youngsters enrolled, between the ages of three and five. We only had to serve them lunch, which they brought from home. The Church provided some milk. I worked now 7 hours daily instead of 12, and the weekends were free, too. I loved the children and they responded in kind. We all spent the cool mornings or rainy days indoors, but on sunny afternoons we used the adjoining playground, complete with sandboxes, a jungle gym and teeter-totter. The nun and I got along well, and I was simply "Schwester Gisela" to all.

The mail became more unreliable every day, and letters from Berlin and the front were often lost. Mother sent me some powdered soups occasionally, but several times the packages had been damaged with most of the soup powder lost. One day a middle-aged soldier stopped by. He turned out to be Walter's personal aide on furlough. He had come directly from the field hospital and was heading for his home in the Rhineland. He brought me letters from Walter, and also several icons and a samovar, which some grateful villagers had given to Walter as gifts for his treating their sick children. The aide told me of the ever increasing numbers of wounded and dead, and the battles coming ever closer to the hospital. He took a letter from me back to Walter, where I described my change of jobs. He would be angry, since he had counted on me to become his office nurse some day in his private practice. Well, at least I gave him some time now to cope with his disappointment.

On a sunny afternoon in late April, while I was sitting on one of the sandboxes surrounded by little children, I felt suddenly faint. When I came to I was inside, where the strong nun had half-dragged and half-carried me. She let me rest on a long table 'til I felt better. Then she sent me home with my promise to see a doctor.

The medical chief from the children's hospital examined me in his private office the next day. He could not find anything wrong, but nevertheless insisted on a urine sample. A week later he called me. "Frau Doktor, a rabbit test has revealed without any doubt that you are pregnant. Congratulations!"

Timing At Its Worst

April 1944 to December 1944

I t is not possible to adequately describe my feelings when I heard I was expecting a child. The emotions ranged from the height of happiness and wonder to the depth of despair and fear. But they all had one thing in common: the determination to do everything in my power for the two of us to survive—somehow.

By showing a physician's certificate of pregnancy to the food stamp office, expectant mothers were granted somewhat improved food allowances, especially desperately craved sugared fruit juices. I also was permitted to quit work within a month, which was a great relief because I was nauseous most of the time. The Nazis realized that the combination of hunger, siren-interrupted nights, long work hours, and the unceasing stress of war would take its toll on the unborn and newborns. After all, the German Reich wanted lots of "healthy, pure-blooded children for its glorious future." And of course, if you were going to conquer the whole world you needed to plant "racially pure" conquerors everywhere. You also needed to replace all the war casualties...

Needless to say, I was embarrassed to find myself pregnant under a regime that daily urged women to produce fresh blood for the fatherland. But, embarrassed or not, I took full advantage of every survival means for us two.

June 5, 1944, was my 19th birthday and first wedding anniversary. I was able to stay home now. My little radio on the rolltop desk played popular tunes, and my girlfriend Hedwig and I danced a little in the living room. On the next day there was an announcement of the Allied invasion of the French coast at Normandy!

I was horrified about the reportedly heavy losses, which were recounted daily. Nevertheless, the invasion seemed to have been successful. I thanked God and the Allies from the bottom of my heart for this light at the end of the tunnel.

In July, my parents started their three-week vacation at Odi's husband's family home in Wildbad, which is a pretty little spa in the impressive Black Forest. The latter stretches all the way from west of Stuttgart to the French border. There, Helmut's mother and his brother Gustav with wife Tina owned and ran a more than 200-year-old resort hotel by the name of Goldener Stern. I joined them there, and Hans, too, would come from Berlin for the last week of our stay.

My parents were delighted, yet also concerned, about my pregnancy. They cautioned me not to wander too far up the steep, thick pine forests. My nausea having abated by now, I became totally addicted to daily hikes, which I began by taking the cable cars that glided up and down the nearest mountainside, loaded with tourists.

The meals were beautifully served in the large wood-paneled dining hall of our hotel, where Gustav and Tina—despite the busy summer season—took the very best care of us. Each guestroom had high, hand-carved wooden beds with overstuffed feather quilts, and all rooms featured balconies brimming with flowers.

At the Wildbad spa in the Black Forest with my parents in the summer of 1944.

Some of Wildbad's immaculately kept dark-wooden houses crept partly up the tight ring of mountains. They reminded me of Swiss or Bavarian chalets with their low, overhanging roofs and carved, flower-laden balconies. On Sundays, various churchgoers would wear their colorful folk costumes, with the women sporting high hats with a large red pompom on top. The area's artisans hand-produced and shipped the world-famous Black Forest pendulum clocks. Many of them featured cuckoos that announced the hours, or costumed couples stepping in and out of their little doors at regular times.

As I was walking near my parents in the spa area one day, a woman approached me, stretched out her hand, smiled and said, "Gisela, don't you recognize me?" I focused on an elderly gaunt and thin face. Then I realized that she was one of the most fanatic Nazi teachers from my last school in Berlin who had been deliberately unfair and nasty to me, and whom I had so feared and despised. My beginning smile disappeared. I stared at her smiling face and outstretched hand. Then I shook my head slowly, turned and walked away.

Despite being warned not to wander off too far, our host's Dalmatian dog, who loved escorting me, and I did manage to get lost! I had climbed all the way up the wooded mountainside opposite from the cable cars to explore the pine forest there with its bountiful ferns and wildflowers. The dog's presence gave me a sense of security, and I was sure he would guide me back. But it turned out that he relied totally on MY sense of direction.

To return from the top, I now slowly and carefully clambered and slid downhill on hundreds of slippery, moss-covered rocks. When I finally emerged from the forest I stared at the valley in front of me—no Wildbad, no houses, no humans—just a meadow with a bubbling brook ringed by the dark green mountain wilderness. I retraced my steps, which meant climbing back up all the way to the summit. By now, even the dog was panting hard and resting frequently. I tried not to panic, but could not help thinking of the tourists who had occasionally gotten lost and died in these endless dark ranges. Then I found a small footpath. I sat down on it, hoping that someone—sometime—would use it.

It was getting dark, which during Germany's summers does not occur 'til about 10:00 PM. Suddenly the dog pricked up his ears and growled. A man in a green uniform approached. He was the area's government forester who was walking his beat to check for game or wood poachers. As we neared the town, two policemen came toward us. They were looking for me, guided by two reliable German shepherd dogs, who were smartly following my scent.

A few days later I picked up Hans at the railroad station. His 17th birthday was just a few days away on July 24. He had grown taller than six feet by now, and was so slender and handsome even in his ill-fitting uniform. His perfectly chiseled face was tanned, his eyes dark and large with long lashes. His deep-brown hair was still wavy, despite his many attempts to straighten it. I noticed with pride that every girl we passed gave him admiring glances.

We were so happy to be together again. We talked while we hiked for miles, and we ate every meal with our parents at the hotel. The nights were restful too, because no sirens howled. The nearest city, Pforzheim, was only mid-sized, non-strategic, and 50 miles away. It had not been bombed yet.

On July 20 we were all seated, along with many other hotel guests, in the large dining room, eating dinner. The radio was playing classical music. Suddenly the program was interrupted with an important news brief. Everyone stopped eating, and then came the announcement that "a dastardly attempt has been made in Munich to assassinate the Führer." Father, Mother, Hans, Gustav and I stared at each other tensely, yet with a glimmer of hope. But the announcer went on to say that Hitler was not injured, and that the would-be assassins would be caught and punished shortly.

There was total silence in the dining hall now, lasting long after the announcement. No one looked at each other. Then Father and Mother took us upstairs to their room, where we prayed that the coup attempters would not be caught, tortured and killed.

While there had been a number of attempts on Adolf Hitler's life, the most noted and reported was the bomb attempt on July 20, 1944. It was later learned that theologian Dietrich Bonhoeffer of the Confessing Church had some involvement. Since Bonhoeffer chose to take a more clandestine and private presence in these activities, it is unlikely that others, like Pastor Harnisch, would have known.

"The Gestapo report on Bonhoeffer described him as 'completely in the opposition.' Still, even after the failure of the July 20, 1944, attempt to kill Hitler, it was months before the Nazis realized the extent of Bonhoeffer's involvement in the resistance circles."

In the next few days more and more arrests were made. My parents knew some of the nobility families involved. We cried for them and for the fact that the unspeakable Nazi leadership would continue to kill Jews and dissidents, and would further steep the whole world in this bloody war.

My parents went back to the horror city Berlin. Hans spent one more day with me in Gmünd before he had to leave for the Russian front. How we hated to say good-bye! We promised to write to each other frequently, but we knew how unreliable the mail was now. Then he was gone and I was alone again.

There was one consolation, though. Within a few days the grapevine and then the radio brought the news that the Allies had liberated Paris!

Walter wrote occasional elated letters from the Russian front, with many suggestions for proper behavior during my pregnancy, especially in regard to smoking. I must admit I was still smoking, but since cigarettes were almost impossible to come by, I was not really worried about the affect on the baby. His parents also offered lots of good advice but no food. My own family in starving Berlin was barely surviving. So I supplemented my meager rations by bicycling uphill for miles to isolated villages, where I traded silverware for a few eggs, some milk, or a piece of smoked ham. This was tricky, because getting caught by ever-watchful Nazi spies meant heavy fines or prison for the farmers and myself.

One day in September I received a letter from a former fellow pediatric nursing student. Her name was Bertha, and she had belonged to the group supported by the Nazi party. We had not been particularly close. She had graduated in the spring and left Gmünd. In the letter she asked me urgently to visit her. She wrote that she was sick, and that there was something important she wanted to discuss with me. Her address was Ulm, a city that lies about 100 miles southeast of Stuttgart.

I hesitated, because I was six months pregnant and train travel was getting unreliable. Also, Stuttgart, where I would be changing trains, was being bombed even at daytime now. But the matter had to be serious or she would not have contacted me.

All went well with the trip. Ulm is a beautiful old city with a famous gothic cathedral. I had never been there before, and in normal times this would have been an interesting tour. But these times were not normal. No cabs, not even streetcars were in service because the tracks had been torn up by bombs. I walked over a mile to reach her apartment.

She was barely recognizable. In Gmünd she had been a rather hefty girl, cool and self-possessed. But now she was emaciated, pale and depressed. Her dark eyes brimmed with tears as she embraced me and thanked me for coming.

She spoke only in whispers and she begged me to lower my voice, also. To the best of my recollection this is what she said:

"Gisela, I have tuberculosis but am afraid to go to a hospital. No, don't try to change my mind. Please just listen.

"After I graduated, the party sent me to a military hospital in Austria, where I was assigned to a surgical ward. As you know, our training had been pediatric, but I adjusted and learned quickly. The work was hard, the hours long. But the food was good, the nurses friendly, the wounded soldiers grateful. Yet there were so many horribly maimed and urgent cases. Oh God, the screams, the blood, the many deaths, the weeping families...I tried to steel myself but did not manage it very well.

"Some medical and surgical supplies were running short. It seemed to me that soldiers with several missing limbs, and those with other severe injuries, were developing too many infections as time went on. So many died before even reaching the operating room. I began to wonder why these men had not been treated sooner—that is, closer to the front in field hospitals. Even if those could not handle these many serious cases, why had they not been sent for quicker help to Poland or Czechoslovakia, instead of being transported all the way to this hospital in a suburb of Vienna? I began to ask myself if this hospital was truly meant to help these men, or if 'our grateful fatherland' had decided to save on medications, food and care for those who would be healthier future prospects!

"I began to watch especially the actions of the two head nurses on our floor. When I was on night duty I started to spend more time in the rooms and halls of the severely injured arrivals. Sure enough, I was sent out repeatedly on small errands by the night head nurse, and inevitably several of these men were dead before morning! When I became ill myself it was almost a relief, because I am on extended leave now from that place of horror.

"Gisela, I was brought up to believe in the greatness of the Führer, the moral righteousness of National Socialism, and the just cause of this war. But I know now that you and your family and other resisters were right. I am so ashamed of this horrible government, of myself, of the whole country. There is nothing I can do to stop the mass-murder of our soldiers in that hospital. I would be killed if I would go public. In fact, no newspaper would touch this story anyway.

"I may be dying, but I think I have a better chance of living longer by not being in hospitals where I, too, may be considered to be dispensable...

"Gisela, you cannot speak of these things to anyone. I know that. But at least I got this horror off my chest, and maybe some day you will let the world know how truly evil fascism really is."

There were few letters from Hans from the Russian front. I was so worried about him. In his notes he sounded depressed and exhausted. I could not protect my little brother anymore, despite my promise to him when we were small. I raged inwardly, How dared any government send its country's men into fighting and death? I swore I would be a pacifist 'til the day I died. Why had the Allies waited so long before they stopped Hitler? Why not use isolation, embargoes and other pressures before he was armed to the teeth, and before this megalomaniac started to swallow up other countries? Why not stop all ruthless dictators peacefully but forcefully early in their tracks? But I knew that humans would always admire and respect their warring heroes rather than their peacemakers. And I also knew the immense power of greedy industrialists whose fortunes increased hugely with wars, and who formed powerful alliances with the military and ruthless politicians.

But where, I wondered, were the mothers in all this? Were not women supposed to be the nurturers? Why did they so carefully and lovingly bring up their babies and young children with vitamins, proper foods, medical care, lullabies, good schools, and church teachings of loving one's fellow man? Just to have their children grabbed and forced to fight and kill other mothers' sons, and then to die themselves in agony? Where had all these loving mothers been throughout history's slaughters? Why did these loving women never stop the carnage of their sons before it was too late?

Would now, at least, a lesson be learned from this hell? Would the world have to get along, without nations and races hating each other? Would war be finally outlawed forever?

I trembled as I stood by the window, watching 12- and 13-year-olds walking by or on bikes, guns slung over their shoulder. They were being trained to "protect the fatherland and their families" at the nearby garrison.

One late day in October while I had a check-up from Dr. Finger, the skilled chief surgeon at the downtown hospital, I looked in, as I often did, on some of the more severely injured soldiers. An air force major was introduced to me by one of the nuns. His entire family, consisting of his wife and three children, had been killed during a bombing raid on the city of Darmstadt. They had not seen each other for months, and he was not able to attend their funeral, either. He had been piloting a supply plane to and from Africa. His plane was shot down, and although he ejected in time, his right arm was shattered. To save the arm, Dr. Finger scheduled several operations and skin grafts. But the arm was infected, with puss showing through the bandages, giving out a putrid odor. He suffered excruciating pain. I began to visit him daily and was happy when his agonized face lit up at my appearance. His name was Georg. He was about 30 and darkly handsome. We talked of our families and our worries and loneliness. I held his hand tightly when he cried about his awful loss.

Soon after another operation he was well enough to walk around some, and finally to dress with my help. We walked outside on the hospital grounds and eventually in the marketplace. There he sometimes stood patiently in the endless food lines in front of a store for me, while I sat on a nearby bench. I was seven months pregnant now, and grateful for his support.

Father wrote that Hans's cavalry regiment had been caught off-guard by a Russian attack, which had left the surviving men scattered in all directions. Hans was slightly injured and ran a fever. But all field hospitals were full. He was given a pass for a rest period in Berlin. But the troop trains were full, too. Hans had hung on to one of the surviving horses, and he rode this horse now all the way back to Berlin. He stopped shortly at inns along the way. He rode for seven days, with his fever rising. But he did reach Berlin, where he was now hospitalized. He was in poor but not critical condition. I thanked God for his being safe for now, anyway.

Georg went through another operation, but then he began to visit me at home. I was so glad not to be all alone anymore, and he enjoyed the non-clinical surroundings. He taught me how to play several card games, especially solitaire. We read and talked and ate some of his hospital food.

He even brought me some tea once, which I happily brewed for us. We also went for walks in the park, being fully aware that the neighbors would be gossiping.

Then one evening we kissed. I don't know why it happened, it just did. I felt safe when he embraced me. We needed each other's closeness. Then we began to make fantastic plans. After the baby was born, and he had the last of his operations behind him, he would be able to fly again. He would steal a plane and we would fly to a country in Africa that was not involved in the war. He knew the routes well. And the three of us would spend the rest of our lives in the jungle, as far away from humanity as possible. At least from white humanity...

We did not have intercourse. He was much too protective of the baby. We sometimes spent the nights together, just happy in each other's company. But we made sure he still spent most of his time at the hospital.

About the middle of November I heard from Hans himself. He was well now and had been ordered to report to Bamberg in South Germany, about 150 miles northeast of Gmünd. He would be able to visit me for a couple of days en route.

I was so glad to see him. He was thinner than ever, and had aged from his ordeal. He was quieter and I knew he was scared. Oh God, how I feared for his life! He was afraid for me and the baby, too. We tried to comfort each other that the war could not last too much longer. Despite the harsh winter weather, the Allies were cleaning northern France of the entrenched German troops and were heading for the Rhine. The Russians were pushing the snow-bogged German army back toward Poland. And German cities were increasingly devastated by bombs. Even Pforzheim, the midsized city near Wildbad, had been almost totally eradicated. Rumor had it that the Germans had erected an imitation clock tower there, which resembled the tall and famous clock tower near Stuttgart's railroad station, in order to keep strategic Stuttgart with its many munitions factories from being recognized by bombers. The ruse worked at least temporarily, and Pforzheim was sacrificed...

Hans and I recounted the accumulating German defeats everywhere. We were sure it would only be a matter of months now before the war would be over. I suggested that he hide in my cellar. The only people who would be aware of his presence would be the upstairs anti-Nazi clergy family, who would never give him away. But Hans said, "Gisela, you are my sister. Yours would be the very first place to be searched from top to bottom if I deserted. We would both be hung from the nearest lamp post." I knew he was right. We all had heard many reports of deserters having been hung by the SS as a warning to would-be deserters. Yet my brain was feverishly searching for some way to keep him safe 'til the war's end, but neither of us could think of a solution. We embraced and kissed as we said good-bye at the railroad station, and I waved through my tears as the troop train pulled out.

It was the end of November 1944. Winter had arrived early and with a vengeance all over Europe. It snowed almost daily. The icy winds tore at my face and clothing as I stood in the long food lines at the few open stores in the market downtown. Germans are always rude and impatient in any line to this day, and they were particularly bad-tempered then. When I finally made it into the store, I stared in disbelief at what was left in there, and I was lucky if I was handed my weekly ration of two eggs, one loaf of bread, a small piece of meat, a pint of milk, a little lard, my fruit juice and lots of old and partially frozen carrots and cabbages. In the summer we had at least received some fruit, but the rhubarb was almost uneatable without sugar.

There was also very little coal to be had for my two pot-bellied stoves. I let the bedroom get cold and slept in the living room. This also helped me to save a few pieces of coal for the baby's arrival. Finally, each household was assigned a few logs of wood. A Czech prisoner of war, who, along with forced laborers from occupied lands, was encamped in the garrison at the end of my street, split the logs in the little garden. I used the pieces for my tiny cook stove, but dared only to use them for one meal per day. The Czech and I were unable to communicate, but he gratefully accepted a little bread from me, and a hot cup of chicory "coffee."

To prepare for the baby's arrival, I tore up and sewed pieces of bed linen for diapers. Hedwig and several other student nurses stole for me some baby clothes from the pediatric hospital, as they had promised me to do when the time drew near. I was ready.

There had been no communication from my parents and Odi for quite some time now. At least Georg spent as much time as possible with me, while daylight hours lasted only from 10:00 AM until 5:00 PM. I knew that troops everywhere were suffering terribly in this cold, snowy winter, and the survivors in the big cities, also. Nazi propaganda was still cranking out phrases such as "strategic withdrawals" and "vital victories." The German people were constantly admonished to continue their "brave efforts to defeat the enemies of the Reich." They were warned that if Germany should ever be defeated (a word not mentioned heretofore), the enemy nations would kill most of the population and would divide our country in tiny pieces among themselves. Less and less people seemed to believe in victory any more, and the faces looked grim now. But they still believed fanatically in the rightness of their cause.

Suddenly, in early December, my mother stood at my door. Her visit was totally unexpected. She was drained of all energy, especially from the hike through the snow from the railroad station while carrying a heavy suitcase. I put her to bed immediately. She talked of the terrible conditions in Berlin, of Odi's being three months pregnant now, while Helmut was somewhere at the Russian front. She told of Father's continuous efforts to help and comfort his parishioners. He had even designed a primitive coal-heating device for apartments that used little coal and somehow filled hot water into clay-tiled cylinders along the walls. Radiators had long been cold in all of Berlin's apartments, of course. He had turned our "salon" into a small factory, where he and parishioners produced these devices, to be used throughout the parish by freezing people.

Father in "workshop" where he designed simple heating devices for his parishioners. The heating device begins at the bottom of the photo—the small "oven" and the long concrete and brick "ducts" that run from left to right.

She also described in detail all the difficulties of her train trip to me. I tried to appreciate the effort, and knew she planned to be helpful after the baby's arrival. But Mother had always insisted on doing things her way, and she was quick to criticize. She would also need at least as much care as the baby because of her weak heart. And then there was the possibility of her finding out about Georg…I called him quickly and he stayed away now. Well, at least Mother had brought some clothes for the baby from my own childhood.

About four days after Mother's arrival, on December 7, I went into labor. It was evening and the ambulance took Mother and me to the downtown hospital. A private room had been readied for me, complete with a baby's crib. It was right next to the delivery room, and as I was wheeled in there I spotted Georg in the hallway, who was smiling at me reassuringly.

Labor lasted all night and into the morning. The ugly old midwife, who sported a big, black wart right on top of her nose, and my hectic mother, stayed close by me. I thought the agony would never end. Then I felt the baby's head stuck and I yelled at the two women to please call the chief surgeon, who had occasionally looked in, but was busy right now in the operating room. He raced to my side, saw my flesh tearing and the cord wrapped around the baby's neck—then I was mercifully put to sleep.

When I awoke I was in my room, with the baby's crib close to my bed. Dr. Finger was congratulating me for a healthy baby boy. He helped me to sit up in bed and look into the crib. There he was—a tiny, red, wrinkly, helpless, soundly sleeping little human being. My very own Michael.

Dr. Finger then explained that the tangled umbilical cord had not harmed the baby. Michael's head was unusually large and got stuck so that I tore badly. Had he been called in earlier he would have prevented the tearing. It took a lot of stitches to sew me up. I thought bitterly, *So much for the acclaimed German midwifery.* I thanked God that Michael and I had survived all the bungling. Except for the forceps' indentations on his head he looked perfectly fine.

As I laid back to rest the door opened and Mother came in. One look at her furious face told me that she must have found out about Georg. She barely glanced at the baby as she threw a piece of unfolded paper and an envelope at me. I stared at his handwriting: "Gisela, congratulations on Michael's birth. I am so happy that you both are all right. I stayed close to you throughout your painful night. I am giving this note to the midwife to give to you after you wake up. Thank God all went well. All my love! Georg."

Gisela with baby Michael

Needless to say, the next few weeks—which should have been the happiest of my life—were pure hell. The miserable midwife had opened the envelope, read the letter, and given it to my mother instead of me. I won't go into details of my mother's accusations and threats. She wanted to write to my husband. I tried to keep calm and reminded her that Walter was in great danger at the front, and needed only happy news about the birth of his son. It would be up to me to tell him or not to tell him some day about Georg, who had been a great help and comfort to me and had never touched me sexually. But Mother would not be soothed, and I suffered endless tirades and her conviction that I would be punished in hell for all eternity.

Her voice was piercing and the midwife was a vicious gossip. By now the entire hospital was enjoying the story of the bad doctor's wife.

Coming home was a nightmare, also. The beds were unmade, no food prepared or dishes done, the rooms were ice cold, and Mother was running around in circles, greeting well-wishers unkempt and in an old, frayed bathrobe. After two weeks she decided to leave. I carried her suitcase to the railroad station and listened to her intentions to fill everyone in as soon as she reached Berlin. Oh well, at least little Michael could get my undivided attention now.

Of Horror and Hope

January 1945 to April 1945

During the winter of 1944 to 1945 the war raged on all over Europe. In France, Hitler's generals made a last desperate attempt to break through the American lines. But on December 16, in a fierce battle that took place in the Ardennes Forest between Belgium and Luxemburg, the incredibly brave American troops managed to stop the German onslaught despite heavy losses. The Allies named this the Battle of the Bulge because the area looked like a bulge on the map.

In the Balkans, the Russians had driven the Germans out of Romania and Bulgaria, and Hitler had pulled his troops out of Greece and Yugoslavia. But German troops were still in Hungary and its capital, Budapest, until February.

In Russia itself, the winter had defeated Hitler as it had once defeated Napoleon. His army was pushed back to Poland, where remnants of the Polish army had risen up against the Germans, with heavy loss of life, until Stalin finally entered Warsaw in January.

Much of this was, of course, not officially announced, but thousands of returning wounded soldiers could not be forced to keep silent.

No one was given leave anymore, either, and mail became a thing of the past. Right after New Year's I'd received one more note from Hans, stamped in Bamberg. Then silence. All mail had ceased from Walter, too, after he had written a happy response to the birth of his son. There was silence from Berlin, also, and from friends and relatives everywhere. Long distance phone service was stopped for civilian use, because bombing had disrupted just about all communications by now.

My greatest concern was the baby's survival. I was nursing Michael, but to my horror the milk was drying up, despite my desperate use of a breast pump. I could not get enough formula on my ration card, either, and was beginning to despair. Then I had a brilliant idea. I asked my nursing student friends at the children's hospital to find healthy new mothers there, and ask them to use breast pumps after they had fed their own newborns, so they could let me have all excess milk. My friends enthusiastically complied, with Hedwig bringing me a fresh supply of mother's milk every evening. And so my little son not only survived but thrived. In fact, he slept soundly even through the wailing of the air raid sirens and the frequent nights spent in the cellar.

Georg adored little Michael and babysat while I sledded downhill into town for errands. It was a meager

Christmas and a quiet arrival of 1945, but just to survive was a daily gift.

In the middle of January my sister Odi moved in with Michael and me. Her pregnancy, which was four months along, had gotten her a train travel permit. She had been without news from her husband Helmut for two months, and the heavy bombing of Berlin had convinced her and my parents that she should save herself and the unborn child. Odi had left my parents behind with a heavy heart, but they would not be moved away from their suffering parishioners, who needed them so badly.

Her arrival was totally unexpected, of course, but I was glad to shelter her. Yet I knew that my privacy would be shattered for good now.

Soon after my sister came to me, she asked to meet the much-discussed Georg. They went for a long walk, from which she returned alone with the announcement that he had promised her to stop seeing me.

I called him and we met. It was a cold, clear, moonlit night. The snow was glistening and crunching under our feet as we walked along the familiar paths in the deserted park. I cried as we sat on a bench with his good arm warm around me. I begged him to wait for me—that I would get a divorce from Walter as soon as the war was over. But we both knew the uncertainty of any future for us, since he could be forced soon to rejoin his squadron, and since my sister had moved in with me now. And so we separated, but we knew we would never forget.

Odi and I got along better than I had thought. We had so much to talk about, so much in common. Our personalities and preferences were different as always, but we soon discovered that two opposite halves can make a useful whole. For instance, she still hated all exercise and loved

Odi sewed her gown from a pair of
drapes. I wore my wedding gown.

quiet, creative activities. Sewing, which I hated with a passion, was one of her many talents. I watched with amazement as she transformed several brightly patterned tablecloths, a pair of drapes, and some sturdy white bed linen into beautiful summer dresses and suits for us, and also knitted and sewed clothes for Michael and her unborn.

In the meantime I cleaned, cooked, and ran errands—always on the move, always quick and decisive, always energetic. We took turns caring for baby Michael, whose crib stood next to the big double bed, which Odi and I now shared.

Our food rations had been cut again, and we were only allowed one egg per week of late. We laughed when our personalities showed their difference even in eating that one precious egg. Odi would make hers last as long as possible by mixing it with some ugly grey looking flour and water, resulting in about six "pancakes" that she rationed to last her about three days. I boiled or scrambled mine and devoured it all at once.

I still resented her many attempts to dominate me, but I also had to admit that some of her advice was useful. And we both knew, of course, that we had to make the best of the situation.

It was February now. During the long evenings I read books to her while she sewed. Or we listened to dance music on the radio and sang with the tunes we knew. But the unrelenting cold was hard to bear. Our coal supply for the two pot-bellied stoves was dangerously low. In the "kitchen" we sometimes found Michael's diapers, which we had soaked overnight, solidly frozen in their bucket. We needed more wood pieces for the two-burner stove to boil the diapers clean and to cook. So we decided to steal some wood.

On a clear day, my friend Hedwig babysat with Michael while Odi and I headed for the nearest hilly woods with my sled. We found very few small branches because the freezing townspeople had cleared out all underbrush. Suddenly we came upon a neatly stacked pile of logs. We knew they were meant to be sold by the government in rationed amounts. Stealing them was punishable by heavy fines or even imprisonment, but we were just desperate enough to chance it. We laid some of these precious logs evenly on the sled, covering them with twigs and my coat. Then Odi sat on top while I pulled the sled down the gently sloping road toward town.

As we rounded a bend we suddenly faced a forester. We returned his friendly greeting and were almost past him when a log dislodged on one side and peeked out in front, because the road had become steeper. He saw it and stopped us. Before he could say much we turned on our tears and told him of baby Michael being so cold at home, and of Odi's pregnancy (which was just beginning to show). We were good and decent pastor's daughters, who never broke the law and would be perfectly willing to pay for the logs. Then we smiled at him through our tears and watched his male ego being flattered by the thought that he would be a knight in shining armor, aiding two pretty damsels in distress. He stopped checking out the logs and let us go with a warning. He even helped us to hide the indiscreet log.

Odi convinced me that we ought to get little Michael baptized, regardless of the absence of relatives. My friend, the kind, white-haired Lutheran clergyman Pastor Teufel who lived in the other half of the manse, agreed that the times were too dangerous to wait for "pomp and circumstance." So I dressed the baby in my own christening gown, which Mother had brought me, and Pastor Teufel baptized him in my living room. I named him simply "Michael" with no middle name at all, while the pastor's wife, Odi, and Hedwig witnessed the Baptism. I could not help wondering, though, if our loving God would have condemned baby Michael to roast in eternal hellfire had a bomb killed him before he was baptized.

The Allies east and west were racing toward Germany now, and all remnants of German troops were needed to try to stem the tide. So the two garrisons at both ends of town had only skeleton military crews left. They were busy training a few handfuls of 12- to 14-year-old youngsters to stay behind and defend the town if necessary. Rumor had it that despite dire threats, some of the departing soldiers had deserted and fled into hiding.

One day in early March Odi decided to do the downtown shopping because I had a cold. To my horror she came home with two young men in tow who were in civilian clothes but were army deserters from one of the garrisons. They had been helpful while she stood in food lines, and had offered to carry the groceries home for her. While they walked they had carefully tested each other on political opinions, and soon trust was established. So now I stared at two young strangers needing me for asylum 'til the end of the war.

I did not consent immediately, of course, because of the danger that Odi and I and even Michael might be executed right along with the deserters. We spent many hours discussing all our fears and possibilities. They promised they would stay totally hidden and not even go down into the cellar for air raids. They both had hidden a duffel bag in the woods, containing their uniforms and some much needed food. They had stolen the latter from the garrison kitchen before they fled. The two were friends and had planned their escape for a long time. Since deserters were surely not expected to hide out in close proximity to the garrison, we all agreed that they would probably be safe in our house. Also, the German military was presently much too busy to search for every deserter. I felt I had to try to save their lives, and so I gave my consent. But how I wished daily that one of them could have been my brother Hans.

Their names were Kuno and Hugo. Both had been university students before they were drafted. Kuno had planned to become a physicist and was the only son of a professor's family in Mannheim. He was an agnostic introvert, and loved debating religion and philosophy. Hugo was an outgoing, friendly medical student from a large family in Hannover. His optimistic outlook on life was a relief in our crammed little household. The two young men stayed inside all day, but took long walks at night in the pitch-darkness of the blackout. They slept on the couch and on the floor in the living room. We all lowered our voices, and if the upstairs anti-Nazi clergy family ever suspected anything they kept it to themselves.

Odi and I knew that our husbands and Hans were somewhere in the middle of chaos on the eastern front. And sure enough, soon a dreaded army telegram arrived, hand-delivered by a soldier. It was three days old. Odi turned ashen and I thought mainly of Hans. But it was addressed to me as follows: YOUR HUSBAND DR. MED. WALTER

D. SERIOUSLY WOUNDED. HOSPITAL HAMELIN. VISIT REQUESTED. TRAVEL PERMITTED HEREWITH.

My first thought was Michael. Could I leave him while I undertook this dangerous trip to North Germany? What if my husband was dead already and I abandoned the baby for nothing? What if Gmünd got bombed while I was away? Or what if I got killed and left Michael motherless? Odi, Kuno and Hugo advised me not to leave. But even though I did not love my husband I thought it was my duty to comfort him and ease his pain, and that he had a right to my presence. So with a heavy heart I left Michael in Odi's and our friends' care, packed a few clothes, and began what turned out to be an incredible odyssey.

I knew full well that I had been able to live in relative security and comfort since I had left Berlin in 1943. But what I now experienced was worse than anything I had imagined. To portray the journey in the exact order of events is impossible. But it all happened.

Hamelin—of "Pied Piper" fame—is a small town in northwestern Germany. Normally the trip would have taken about five hours, but now it took me five days and nights to reach the town, and it seemed miraculous that I even got there at all. Stuttgart's main railroad station was already in rubble. A few trains left from a suburb, but only after dark. I heard that daytime traffic attracted British Spitfire planes, which were located in fairly close-by France now. My fellow passengers were mainly soldiers and very few women. Train travel was possible only for short distances because of bombed-out tracks. We were time and again loaded into occasional army vehicles, if they had room left in them. Or we hiked in groups along tracks until there were trains available again. The March weather was still cold and clammy. I was wet, hungry, and very tired. Once, on a moonlit night, the truck on which I was riding—while crowded together with others like sardines—was suddenly attacked by a Spitfire. In the nick of time the driver managed to steer us off the road and into a stand of trees, where we waited tensely for hours 'til we felt safe enough to proceed. On the third day or so I had reached the city of Darmstadt by train at dawn, where we pulled into a small suburban station to await the nightfall. All passengers were ordered to leave the train and rest in a nearby bomb shelter. Even though I was dead tired, sleep would not come. I rose and stood by the entrance, looking at the sun rising over the city of Darmstadt only a couple of miles away. Suddenly air raid sirens howled from all directions, and a few minutes later I heard bombs bursting and saw buildings exploding and large clouds of smoke rising from the city. I felt nauseous and my heart was racing. I lay down and covered my ears. After a few hours of fitful sleep I awoke from the sound of machine gun fire. Some of us peeked out the entrance door just in time to see a Spitfire raking our empty train with bullets, flying directly the whole length of it. We all hit the floor. None of us were hurt, but our train was totally disabled, and when dark finally came we trudged on by foot. Our conductor eventually found a train and a crew to take us a little ways northward again.

The town of Hamelin had several hospitals like Gmünd, and was therefore spared the bombing. I found my husband, but before I went to his room I was referred to his surgeon, who described Walter's injuries to me. Evidently his last frontline hospital somewhere in Poland had been blown up by grenades. He had a gaping wound in his belly, so emergency surgery was performed on him and he was put on a hospital ship bound for Germany via the Baltic

Sea. While approaching a German harbor, the ship was bombed and sunk, with most of the wounded drowning. Walter, who was a poor swimmer, grabbed a floating object and was eventually rescued and flown to this hospital in critical condition. He had undergone three operations already and was upgraded to "serious" now.

He was still in too much pain to communicate much with me. I spent several days in his room, where a cot had been placed for my use. His fever went gradually down. I helped with his care, but when he felt better I argued with him because he insisted that I stay there. I explained to him my urgent need to return to Gmünd and Michael, but he was not listening. Suddenly he blurted out, "You cannot leave me because the Allies will come here soon, and I will be imprisoned and maybe even executed. I need you because of your family's well-known resistance to the Nazis. You may be able to save me!" I thought at first that he was still delirious and tried to convince him that the Allies were not brutal SS men and that he would not be imprisoned for life, much less killed just because he had been an officer, and a medical one at that. But he kept on pleading with me to stay. Suspicion began to form in my mind. Was there something in his past that he had hidden from me? I confronted him and heard some of the truth. He had already joined the Nazi party in the gymnasium and all his medical studies at the best German universities had been paid for by the party, who had a right to his services later. He knew that I would never have married him had I known this. I refused to hear anymore, assured him he would be safe where he was, and left.

The return trip southward was another horror saga, with the worst happening ironically just before I reached home. In order to skirt Stuttgart, I had purposely detoured to approach Gmünd from the east rather than the west, preferring the relatively safer small towns along the route. An army vehicle had left me near the railroad yard of Aalen, where I had distributed the leaflets secretly over a year ago. So far, Aalen had not been bombed much. It just happened to become a target the very day I was waiting there for nightfall, to catch the only train to Gmünd. When the air raid sirens sounded I descended into a large public shelter, along with many townspeople and travelers. Then the bombs fell all over the nearby railroad yards. I curled up tightly, shutting my eyes and ears, praying and crying like everyone else around me. A nearby hit caused the ceiling of our entrance to cave in, with rocks pelting me and dust choking me into fits of coughing. Then suddenly there was silence. It was over and I was alive! When the de-warning sirens howled many hands, including mine, moved stones, metal and plaster out of the way until the sun broke through a hole and we lifted each other up and out.

Somehow I reached home a few hours later, exhausted and sobbing. Odi, Kuno and Hugo cried with relief, too, and then I was finally able to hug my baby.

March was drawing to a close. The Allies had crossed the Rhine and were racing toward the Elbe River, while the Russians were advancing in east Germany. We looked forward to the end of the war with great hope and great fear. Would Hitler give up, or would the Nazis poison us all yet, as they had hinted lately, rather than surrender? Even if they didn't, would we all get killed at the end in city-to-city fighting? Would the western Allies get here first or—horror!—the Russians? Would Helmut and Hans get home soon now or be killed?

I had been back from my awful trip about two weeks when the doorbell rang one night. An army ambulance delivered my husband! He was brought in on a stretcher and deposited on the bed, with the doors shut tightly to the living room where Kuno and Hugo were hiding.

The driver and the male nurse told me that Walter had signed himself out of the hospital, against his surgeon's advice. He had paid them a royal sum to drive him here all the way from Hamelin, and they had willingly done so because their families lived in South Germany, also. They had wanted to deliver him to our downtown hospital, but he had insisted on being taken home.

Walter was more dead than alive. His belly wounds had broken open from the terribly long and rough trip. He was in excruciating pain and had taken large doses of morphine. While Odi joined Kuno and Hugo in the living room, I spent the rest of the night in bed with my husband. Whenever he awoke he begged me to hide him here, so that the Allies would not arrest him in the hospital. I prayed for dawn to come and then called Dr. Finger, who immediately ordered the hospital to send an ambulance. He was waiting for us when we arrived, and as fast as Walter could be anesthetized Dr. Finger operated on him. This skilled surgeon, who once had been Walter's chief, along with the devoted nuns, together pulled him through, despite his insane flight.

We had heard of the Yalta conference in February where Churchill, Roosevelt and Stalin had met to discuss which zone of Germany would be occupied by each of their troops, as well as by the French. Now the British and the Canadian troops had come from Belgium and were moving into northwestern Germany. The French and Americans were coming in farther south. So we began to guess that we would end up in either a French or an American zone. I remember Odi and me brushing up on our school French and English. The

Russians, in the meantime, had occupied Vienna and had crossed the Oder River and were heading for Berlin. Most German cities lay in ruins, and there was little or no resistance, except for Berlin, where the Nazis forced the troops to make a last stand. Berlin was totally surrounded by Russian troops on April 25, and Hitler, Göebbels and company committed suicide in their bunker there on April 30. Odi and I did not know this then, but we were little surprised when we heard it. After all, these fanatic madmen were cowards as well.

On May 1, which had always been the great Nazi "Labor Celebration Day," the French had already occupied Stuttgart, where they stopped. The Americans kept going and were now within a few miles of our town Gmünd. The two garrisons were deserted, except for some foreign forced laborers and refugees. There was no sign of the 12- to 14-year-old boys, who were supposed to "defend Gmünd." Now Kuno and Hugo decided to act.

Some time ago they had built a little cart, which they had attached to my bike. Now they put on their army uniforms, grabbed the bike and encouraged some town folk to follow them to their former garrison "for food distribution." Word spread like wildfire and a large throng came along. At the garrison, Kuno and Hugo "ordered" the people to help them break down all gates and doors to kitchens, mess halls, and food storage places, which they had long ago scouted out. Within a few hours everything edible had been carted off, and the foreign laborers and refugees helped themselves, too. Kuno and Hugo came home with lard, flour, canned meat, powdered eggs, and even a small crate of apricot liqueur, which they had found in the officer's mess.

Then we said good-bye. They donned their civilian clothes, took their February-dated marching orders as proof that they were deserters, and simply walked out of the town, toward the American lines, to give themselves up and offer their services. They both spoke English flawlessly.

The next day, May 2, 1945, was a sunny morning in Gmünd. The silence was deafening. Nothing moved, everyone was hiding in their houses, the shops and cellars sealed. I decided to hang up some laundry in back of the house, despite Odi's warning. Suddenly shells exploded into the hillside towards the garrison, some of them quite close to my head. I flew into the house where we grabbed little Michael and raced downstairs into the cellar, where our upstairs neighbors were already assembled. But the attack did not last long, as there was no responding fire from the garrison. I ventured upstairs and peeked through the curtains at the street. They were here! Column after column of camouflaged military vehicles rumbled and drove by my bedroom window on the broad street leading up the hill. In and on them were many American soldiers with guns and helmets. I called Odi who brought Michael up, and we started to laugh and to cry. We opened the window and waved and yelled "Thank you!" and "God bless you!" in our very best school English. A few soldiers looked grim, some looked startled, but many of them smiled and waved back. Once again we were "out of step," but finally without fear of punishment.

The town had been left totally intact. Not a shot was fired, not a building damaged. American soldiers patrolled the streets and occupied the town hall and the police station. The partially military hospital downtown, where Walter was a patient, was permitted to continue its function, but for the time being no one was allowed to enter or to leave, and all German military personnel and patients were screened and declared prisoners of war.

The war was over for Michael, Odi, and me, thank God. And five days later, on May 7, Germany finally surrendered. May 8 was declared V-E ("Victory in Europe") Day, and the Nazi government was history.

Rebuilding From Ashes

May 1945 to Fall 1945

Words cannot describe my relief. It was as if heavy weights had been lifted off me after what had seemed like a nightmarish eternity. I felt terribly sad for mankind's horrendous loss of life, and feared for the countless missing and wounded. But the fall of this evil fascist dictatorship had broken the stranglehold of despair, horror and shame that had suffocated me and many resisters and minorities.

If only we had word from Helmut, Hans and our parents. It had been months, also, since we last heard from Grandmother and her sister in Brieg, near the Polish border. Had Brieg, where Hans and I had learned to swim, been destroyed? Had the two old ladies been able to flee from the Russian troops? If so, had they survived such a flight? And whatever had happened to Uncle Engbert, Mother's youngest brother? Did he get out of Yugoslavia alive? Still so many more questions than answers.

At least we now heard that the Allies had been able to rescue survivors in some of the death camps. Most Germans had not known about the existence of concentration camps. Even my family had not realized how many millions upon millions of Jews and others had been slaughtered in these camps. To our relief we found out that Dr. Martin Niemöller had been rescued by the Allies from Dachau. As mentioned earlier, he had been the courageous leader of the small group of Nazi-resisting Lutheran churchmen and parishioners, of whom my parents had been such brave members. He was in poor health, but he had miraculously survived the death camp.

It was actually long after Germany's surrender before we found out that our parents had survived the bombs and the fighting in Berlin. But their story belongs here in this moment of time.

Amazingly, our area in East Berlin had suffered relatively little bomb damage. Still, hunger and cold had taken its toll there, too, especially among the elderly. As I had mentioned before, Father's invention of home-constructed economy stoves had saved hundreds from freezing to death. But even he had no solution for the hunger. My parents were gaunt and weak like everyone else, but they shared what little they had and were kept alive by occasional help from butchers and bakers in our parish.

When the Russians approached Berlin, the Nazi pastor who lived on the floor below us—the one who had denounced Father to the Gestapo repeatedly—fled from the city, as did many other Nazi puppets and agents.

Now when the Russians came, the city was "defended" street by street by remnants of the German army in Hitler's furious last attempt to repel the "invaders," while the frightened residents hid in the cellars of their apartment houses. During a lull in the fighting my parents went out into our deserted Samariter Street and into the equally deserted neighborhood, which was littered with corpses. They carried and dragged the dead toward the church. Our old family doctor came out and tended to the few who were still alive. Then he helped my parents with carrying the corpses off the street. He wore a white shirt, clearly marked in front and back with a red cross. But suddenly a single bullet hit him and he fell mortally wounded. His family rushed out and carried him inside.

Father and parishioners bury the bodies they picked up on the streets in the church backyard.

Eventually, one by one some of our parishioners ventured out and began to help my parents with moving the dead into the sacristy of the church. There, Father and Mother carefully searched about 50 bodies for their identities. There were several nationalities among them, and my parents carefully collected, tagged and catalogued each body and their belongings. In the meantime, Father had the parishioners dig a large mass grave in the center of the garden plot behind the church, directly under a weeping willow tree. All bodies were laid to rest there, and then Father conducted the funeral service.

Father conducts the funeral service for the unknown dead
buried in the backyard of the church.

Even before the Russians occupied Berlin, many rumors of rape and pillage preceded them. To prepare for the worst scenario, Father stocked the senior center downstairs, which he had created a year ago, with more donated cots and beds so that lone women and girls could find overnight safety there. The rumors turned out to be true, and more and more women had to hide there when darkness fell. Father contacted some Russian military officials and they posted guards at the door of the senior center.

As time went on, the Russians trusted and respected Father increasingly. They knew about his anti-Nazi history and they needed his advice and moral leadership. So, at least for the time being, they often accepted and acted on his complaints about drunken and raping soldiers. They also relied on his advice when they eventually set up a regional provisional government. And, per his request, they even granted him permission and financial aid to rebuild some bombed-out East Berlin churches. He redesigned them into simple but beautiful structures, hired the workers and got the materials. Then he personally supervised all activities with daily visits to every construction site.

Father supervising reconstruction of a bombed out church

Within only one year's time he had reconstructed five bombed-out East Berlin churches!

His bad hip hindered his mobility, of course, so the Russians allowed him to purchase a custom-built motorized three-wheel vehicle, which had a back seat for Mother, and could be driven on the sidewalks if necessary. The parishioners of the bombed-out churches helped to pay for this transportation, and the Russians furnished the gasoline. For a long time his was the only German civilian vehicle visible on the streets.

Father in his three-wheel vehicle

As I said before, Odi and I found out about all this much later. In Gmünd, meantime, the two of us awaited the birth of her baby, which was due in June. Odi had severe backaches in her eighth and ninth months, and was unable to help with chores. But the food supplies that Kuno and Hugo had left us helped to keep up our spirits and health for a few weeks, anyway.

Many United States soldiers were busy now with the various tasks of occupying and supervising Gmünd. After screening all of us, the military government issued photo ID cards, which were required to receive food rations. Refugee families and forced laborers from many nations were trucked to the two garrisons where they received shelter and care under supervision of the United States troops and eventually, the UNRA (United Nations Refugee Administration). All our neighbors up and down our street had to evacuate their large homes and villas because the Americans needed living quarters. But our duplex house was protected because it was a parsonage with two anti-Nazi clergy families in it. The American's hung "Off Limits" signs on the house, and to our huge relief no one ever ordered us to leave the premises.

We were daily thankful that United States rather than French troops were occupying our town. We heard some horror stories about Moroccan troops—who had been fighting for the French—raising hell in Stuttgart with rapes and thefts, without any fear of punishment. But I was sure that nothing, but nothing, could compare to the sadism of Hitler's murderous SS and Gestapo while France and so many other countries were occupied by the Germans.

On June 10, 1945, Odi's beautiful baby girl Regula was born in the civilian part of the downtown hospital. I stayed with her throughout her labor, while a skilled midwife assisted her. All went well, with no complications whatever.

So now we were four of us again in my two-room apartment. No word yet from Odi's husband or from Hans. My own husband, Walter, was still recuperating as a prisoner of war in the military part of the downtown hospital. He sent word to me that he wanted to see me and Michael, and I sent word back that I would walk the child in the street under a certain hospital window every day from about 10:00 AM to 10:15 AM. So, unless it rained, I put six-month old little Michael into the carriage and wheeled him downtown daily, so his father could wave to us from a window.

After the supplies from Kuno and Hugo had run out, the miserable diet I was on suddenly made me develop some very large and painful boils under the right arm, which had to be lanced, cleaned, and sutured. The outpatient surgery was done at the hospital. Dr. Finger operated and Walter assisted. I was anesthetized with sodium pentobarbitone, and when I began to come to I found myself lying on a gurney in an empty physiotherapy room. I was still dizzy and trying to focus on my husband's face as he was bending over me. He was furious and plying me with questions about my "affair" with Georg. A female secretary at the hospital, who evidently had nothing better to do than carry tales to and from the wounded, had "informed" my husband. He had bided his time and now confronted me, knowing the pentobarbitone would loosen my tongue. I am sure he was disappointed about not hearing a lurid sex tale, but hearing instead of my never having loved him at all. Georg had filled my loneliness with warmth and decency and a deep friendship, which had never culminated in bed. I had kissed him—yes. I still missed him—yes. But I had not missed Walter, ever.

Now rage overcame this controlled, church-going, stiff and prim man. He slammed the gurney hard against the wall. I was too weak and delirious to hang on, and thus fell off. And although Walter had seen my fall, he walked out the door. I remember thinking dizzily, Whatever happened to medical ethics? But at the same time relief flooded me that the truth serum had enabled me to speak the truth.

A few days later, all hospital military personnel and patients were evacuated and moved in American trucks to a prisoner of war camp near the town of Göppingen, which is situated about 15 miles southwest of Gmünd. I soon heard through the grapevine that the huge prison camp was humanely run by the Americans, and that my husband had been put in charge of the camp infirmary.

Little Michael and baby Regula were healthy and adorable and bright. But hunger was still Odi's and my greatest concern. I must also admit here that, despite years of tobacco deprivation, we both were still addicted to cigarettes, and we picked up the discarded butts from GIs whenever we spotted them on the streets, just like everyone else in town. We always unpeeled and rolled them into whole cigarettes with the aid of fresh papers and a little machine.

Once, while every German dwelling was routinely searched for weapons—including ours—I enjoyed "surrendering" my husband's decorative but dull parade sword to two friendly United States army officers. I was sure, of course, that they would take it back to America as a souvenir. Then we offered them each a glass of Kuno and Hugo's apricot liqueur. They loved it, and in return for letting them have the pint-sized bottle they offered Odi and me several packs of cigarettes. They came back one day for more liqueur, and this time we got chocolate and K-rations and more cigarettes. We now rationed and spaced our supply of liqueur carefully, which kept us in cigarettes, Spam, and candy bars for several months. Compliments of Kuno and Hugo...

Then one day in August, Helmut stood suddenly at the door. He had not even expected to find Odi here, much less his baby. He had just wanted to find shelter with me before he would go on to Berlin. For a moment Odi and I did not recognize him. His head was shaven down to the scalp, some old, part civilian, part military clothes hung loosely around his terribly thin six-foot-seven-inch frame. He was unshaven, unwashed, and totally exhausted. But he was alive! Before he fell asleep he hugged his wife and his baby girl. He had not even known that Odi was expecting his child when he had to leave her in Berlin well over a year ago.

I will not go into details of his war experiences in Russia, except that he was very lucky to have survived his assignment of tank repairs in the icy Russian landscape of the worst winter in Europe's history. Not to speak of the battles all around him, his final surrender to the Russian troops, or the horrible march to a prison camp near Austria. He and another officer, a female, had escaped from the camp together one night in June. They mainly walked nights and rested days, hiding in ditches and woods, living on what they stole from farms, fields, and orchards until they reached Gmünd over a month later. Odi was not enthusiastic about his rather attractive female companion. But we let her rest before she continued on her way to the Rhineland.

A few days later, Odi and I contacted the local military government and inquired about Helmut's status as an escaped prisoner of war from a Russian camp. After hearing our story and of our parent's anti-Nazi record, they sent an officer with us who interviewed Helmut. The two exchanged and signed a lot of documents, and he was permitted to remain with us. Eventually he got a work-study permit and an ID card. But it took several weeks of bureaucratic snags until he got ration cards.

Our life at home became crammed and complicated. I slept on the couch, with Michael next to me on the two easy chairs, which we had tied together to make a safe bed. Odi, Helmut, and Regula occupied the bedroom.

Highly educated, skilled professional German engineers were in great demand, especially for the ruined railroad industry. With no trucks, cars or gasoline available, trains were absolutely vital for everyone's survival. Helmut found a university in Stuttgart that had opened a branch for professional engineers to specialize in railroading. He and his fellow engineers were provided with a "room" in a railroad car on a siding in Stuttgart. His weekends were spent in Gmünd with us.

Hunger drove Odi and me to desperate measures. We dressed in dark clothes, darkened our faces and hands and—on partially moonlit nights—hiked up our hill toward the mountains. Far off, there was a small village nestled in one of the valleys, with some fields of vegetables on the outskirts. We left the road, stumbling and crouching among lettuce, peas, and seed potatoes, filling a canvas bag that Odi had sewn. The villagers guarded their produce and we were very scared. One night, as we were ready to tiptoe back to the road we heard rustling. We threw ourselves headlong into the ditch by the road, holding our breath. The rustling and breaking of twigs grew louder, and then it stopped. I slowly raised my head and saw the outline of several deer looking down at us. They were as startled as we were, and then they fled. We had spoiled their own plans of vegetable thievery.

A relative of one of Walter's fellow prisoners of war in Göppingen delivered a note to me from my husband, in which he asked me to visit him. I knew that German prisoners of war were not allowed to have visitors, and I was not enthusiastic about seeing him anyway. But a friend of mine wanted to visit his wife who, as an army nurse, was also a prisoner in the camp. So I could count on some help if I needed it. I was also aware that Odi and Helmut needed some privacy, and, admittedly, it was exciting to look forward to an adventure.

So, on a sunny Saturday morning in August the friend and I took off on our bikes for the 15-kilometer ride to the outskirts of Göppingen. It was late afternoon when we approached the camp, which consisted of numerous tents in a wooded area that rose like an island from the flat, bare fields surrounding it. A high fence circled the camp, and a road among the fields was patrolled by United States army jeeps.

We hid our bikes in some bushes and watched and waited 'til the jeep patrol was out of sight. Then we ran across the field and, with my friend's help, I climbed over the fence. Grinning prisoners showed me the way to the largest tent, which housed the infirmary and my husband's quarters.

He was in good health and told me that many prisoners had been screened and released already, and that he had been notified that he would be released in about three weeks. He wanted two favors from me. First, I was to take a resume he had prepared to area hospitals for possible employment after he was released. I knew this would not be an easy task, because there was suddenly a large surplus of medical doctors who were returning from now closed field hospitals everywhere, and who were all looking for hospital placements or for the few available private practices. Secondly, he asked me to smuggle out some medical and light surgical instruments, such as scalpels, for his future use in a private practice. I was horrified at first, because stealing was totally unethical as far as I was concerned, unless it saved lives. But he showed me a huge supply of instruments and convinced me that they would not be needed because the camp was emptying fast. No one had any idea from which German field hospitals all these instruments had come.

To this day, I do not understand exactly why I agreed to do this. Even if it was not wrong, it was a dangerous and therefore stupid undertaking. But somehow I felt I owed him something, at least for having gotten me out of Berlin once.

With the help of a nurse I carefully unraveled the stitches in the hem of my skirt, and several instruments were then sewn into it. The weight felt awkward as I walked, but the consensus was that it looked inconspicuous.

We spent the rest of the night on the two cots, and in silence. I was relieved when at dawn Walter and several prisoners accompanied me to the fence. The road in the adjoining fields showed no activity, and many hands shoved me up the fence. I climbed over the top and then half slid and half jumped down onto the field. When I turned and faced the road a jeep suddenly appeared. I knew it would look even worse if the MPs should see me trying to lay down flat. So I simply stood tall and awaited the approaching vehicle.

The driver and his companion ordered me to raise my hands, which I did. They checked my ID and asked what I was doing there. I realized then that they had not seen me jump, and answered that I was trying to talk to my husband through the fence, who was a prisoner in the camp.

They took me to the guardhouse at the main gate, and an officer questioned me once more. All the while I was praying that I would not be thoroughly searched. A short while later my husband's presence in the camp was confirmed and I was released with a stern warning. I retrieved my bike—ignoring my friend's bike which was still there—and pedaled the long trip home.

On August 6 and August 9, Hiroshima and Nagasaki's tragic atomic destruction had put a horrible end to the war in the Pacific, and Japan signed its surrender on September 2. The worst war in the bloody history of humanity was finally over. Millions had died until the madman and his allies had been defeated. Millions of families all over the globe had lost their beloved members. Millions were missing, millions crippled for life, and millions suffered psychological trauma 'til the end of their days.

There was still no sign of life from Hans. We heard that the Russians had shipped thousands of German prisoners of war as far east as Siberia. As we found out later, all through this summer and fall trains came into Berlin from the east with returning German troops, who had been released by the Russians. Father and Mother—sometimes spelled by friends—went many times to the huge burned-out train station in East Berlin, where the International Red Cross tried its best to reunite families. Long lists were printed daily and listed alphabetically with names of new and old arrivals, but Hans's name was never among them. Whenever another trainload arrived, my parents or friends would hold up a sign with Hans's name on it in the hope that someone among the returning soldiers had met him or might even know where he was, or what happened to him. But there was no response from anyone.

When there were no more troop trains, Father had a small stone fountain built with a marble memorial plate above it. It stood in the corner of the garden behind Samariter Church, and I have seen it several times in my life. But it was many years before I gave up hope, and in my heart Hans remains 17 years old, and he will be with me every moment of my remaining life.

The memorial built for Hans in the little cemetery behind the church.
It is still there today.

Walter was released in September. My search for a medical position for him had been largely unsuccessful. Only the director of the tuberculosis hospital on the hill above Gmünd was willing to wait for my husband's release. To my surprise and dismay Walter did not want to work there because TB was "too contagious." His father then searched and found a position for him as staff physician in a huge old castle, which had been converted into a hospital. It was situated in the village of Stetten, about halfway between Gmünd and Stuttgart. His parents still lived in a village nearby, where they had found refuge from the bombing of Stuttgart.

Before he moved to Stetten he stayed in the downtown Royal Inn, because our apartment was too overcrowded. I did not join him there, and one day he asked me to walk with him so we could have a private conversation.

We went up a wooded hill until we found a clearing with ferns and wildflowers. I unpacked a small lunch, all the while planning to ask him for a divorce. But he wanted to speak first.

He did not apologize, nor did he refer to my statements that I did not love him. Instead he showed me a large sketchbook, which he had carried in his backpack. It featured page after page with his pastel sketches of my "affair" with Georg, as he imagined it. It was artistically and tastefully done, as was all his artwork, but it told the story exactly as he interpreted it: There was the beautiful young bride who walked with her doting husband hand-in-hand through spring-green woods. But the big bad war separated them and he was seen in a field hospital in snowy Russia, while she was sitting by a window at home, weeping and waiting. As she thought her husband was dead, an injured soldier—who was also lonely—met her and they comforted each other. But they remained faithful to their respective spouses, and when the big bad war was over each happily returned to their loved ones. The last sketch showed the reunited couple walking hand-in-hand again—through lush summer woods this time.

I stared dumbfounded at the pictures, which he had drawn during the long evening hours in the infirmary. I sat silent as he "forgave" me now and blamed the war and my youth. He was sure that I had grown up and that we would both forget the whole episode and live happily ever after.

Since I could not decide whether to laugh or to cry I did neither. He reminded me so of his brother, whom I had kissed lightly on the forehead after I had turned down his marriage proposal, and who had also chosen to misinterpret my pity. I realized now that I had probably made a major mistake by remaining friendly after the event in the physiotherapy room.

It was now my turn to speak. I told him I had not wanted to hurt him during his frontline perils, his injuries and his imprisonment. But the truth remained that I had been much too young and naïve when we were engaged and married. We had not really dated or known each other at all, and I had never loved him. I wanted a divorce now, for both our sakes and for Michael's, who should not have to grow up with the horror of feuding parents and an eventual nasty divorce.

He asked me to reconsider. He was sure that in time I would love him. The war had caused our "estrangement" and it was over now. His voice began lecturing again as he reminded me that we were pastor's children and divorce was sinful and totally unthinkable.

As time went by, his calls to me from Stetten—now that regional phone calls were permitted again during certain times of the day—became more urgent, and I dreaded his occasional visits in Gmünd. I was helplessly dependent on him to take the initiative with a divorce for three main reasons. First, his family was very influential in Stuttgart. Divorce courts were jam-packed with post-war estrangements. His father knew several judges and lawyers who could speed up what could be taking years. Second, I had very little money of my own for such an expensive procedure. And last, but not least, was that I needed an amicable divorce rather than having to fight for Michael's custody with a very uncertain outcome.

So I continued being friendly but distant and determined, hoping that he would eventually have to give up and start the proceeding.

His pressure and my crowded home was beginning to make me feel claustrophobic. Odi was pregnant again, and despite Michael's and Regula's sweetness I dreaded having to fight for food for one more of us. A call from Walter gave me a chance to get some apples from him, a whole crate full in fact, if I could manage to get to Stetten to pick it up. His town was not near the railroad, so a neighboring GI, who had occasionally used his jeep to pick up things for us, agreed to drive me to Stetten.

Unless one had an official permit, Germans were not allowed to ride in United States Army vehicles. We waited therefore 'til after dark. He was a lively little guy of Italian ancestry, who was not particularly homesick for his rather poor and crammed neighborhood in New York City. Though my English was slowly improving, listening was still much easier than talking. So I listened as he answered my questions about his fascinating city, while we zoomed along on the snaky, hilly road in the dark at about 40 to 50 mph. He took a curve rather sharply and I was convinced that he would hit the rocky incline on my side. In panic I leaned over and grabbed the wheel, and since I had never driven a car in my life, I over-steered to the left. I felt a crushing blow against my face, and when I came to I was staring at the starlit sky above me, wondering why one could still see stars after one was dead. Then I heard moaning and decided I was still alive and felt searing pains in my face. The moaning came from my GI buddy, who was lying a few feet away from me, also on the shoulder of the road. We called to each other and he thought his legs were broken. He had been ejected through his door, and I through the windshield, when the jeep hit a tree. The car then continued to travel and fell down the embankment onto the railroad tracks below. We would have been dead had we not been thrown clear. We whispered that we must not let on that he had picked me up from home. Instead, I had hitchhiked to get the apples, and he had picked me up because he felt it was not safe for a young woman to stand alone by the highway in the dark. He also insisted that neither one of us should mention that I had taken the wheel, but that he had tried to avoid a deer.

Not long after our talk a troop carrier came along and stopped. The men decided to take us back to Gmünd rather than to wait for an ambulance. We were driven to an American field hospital at the outskirts of town. My friend was sedated and, after interviewing us, they had me sign some papers absolving the United States Army from any responsibility for the accident. I gladly signed everything and then was taken to our downtown hospital, where Dr. Finger, with the use of local anesthetics, painstakingly removed countless glass splinters from my face. Luckily nothing was broken and I had only a slight concussion. He sent me home by ambulance with the order to stay flat in bed for several days.

Because it was a weekend, Helmut was there, too. After I rang the bell I yelled that I was OK and had been in a minor accident. But they were still stunned when they saw me. My face looked absolutely gruesome for several weeks. It was swollen to almost twice its size, with large blue marks over my eyebrows, nose and cheekbones. My eyes were barely visible and the whole face was bloody and painted with red iodine. I forbade visits from anyone, but was finally allowed to sleep in my own big bed, with little Michael's crib next to me. Odi and Helmut grinned as they hung a more than life-sized framed photograph of my former prettier self above the bed. It had originally hung in the store window of the downtown photography studio as an advertisement of their work. And after several months of my fellow townspeople having to look at me daily I was given the portrait free of charge.

Among the few visitors I allowed were Kuno and Hugo. They had traveled once more back to Gmünd from Mannheim, where Kuno worked at a science lab, and where Hugo had decided to take his final medical exam. We celebrated our mutual survival with a glass of apricot liqueur, of course.

They stayed at the downtown Royal Inn and Kuno departed soon. But Hugo suddenly decided to apply for his internship at our hospital, and Dr. Finger accepted him. He visited us occasionally when his busy schedule allowed. I was nearly healed in early October when Dr. Finger called me with the sad news that Hugo had been stricken with appendicitis and had not told anyone about it. After two days the appendix had burst and he had died on the operating table despite Dr. Finger's desperate attempts to save him. I had never before believed in fate as such, but death claiming this young man, after all our efforts to keep him from getting killed, made me wonder.

After his death Odi told me that Hugo had been desperately in love with me from the very beginning. But he had begged Kuno and Odi to keep his secret. He wanted to wait if I was serious about a divorce, and only then would he try to win my heart. Now I understood why he had come back to Gmünd and why he had stayed. I felt even worse now, and strangely guilty.

To get back once more to my jeep accident, our little GI friend did have two fractured kneecaps and was flown back to the United States for intricate surgery. But he somehow talked the ambulance driver, who was taking him to the airport in Stuttgart, into stopping at our house first. Odi, Helmut, and I came out and hugged him and wished him well. He gave us his address in New York should we ever visit there. And he would not let me apologize for having messed up his knees, and maybe even his life.

Did We Learn?

The angry reaction of most Germans to the demise of the Third Reich came as no surprise to me. Their outward hospitality fooled many foreigners, but there was mainly rage, no expression of guilt. Rage about "our defeat," rage about "the Allies outnumbering us," rage about our "inferior, envious enemies," rage about Hitler's "stupid tactical mistakes, without which we would have won."

In our town, as everywhere else, many now fawned pathetically for favors from the victor, while others tried to ignore the "Amis." They watched furiously from behind their lace curtains as fraternization started between American soldiers and German girls.

It was November of 1945. I became increasingly depressed and felt like I was suffocating. My bike had been stolen by refugees one night when I had forgotten to lock it up. Walter kept insisting on resumption of our marriage, and my two-room apartment was stiflingly overcrowded. I yearned for freedom from my countrymen, my relatives, my husband. I wanted out. I wanted to know more about the rest of the world, about myself. I wanted a new life.

Little Michael would be safe for a few weeks with Odi and Helmut. I would be back latest by Christmas. Since there were still no trains in service I was planning on hitchhiking northwards, perhaps going to Berlin to find out if Father and Mother had survived. My English was still sparse, but my grammar was good and I knew I would learn quickly if I conversed enough with GIs. Perhaps I could find a job as an interpreter somewhere and then fetch Michael. And my absence might finally convince Walter to start divorce proceedings.

Odi and Helmut were worried, but they promised to take good care of Michael and to give Walter a brief note

From left to right: Gisela, Helmut (Odi's husband) and Odi, 1946.

for me at his next visit. They gave me letters to my parents in case I made it up there. Then we hugged and cried a little and I left.

What followed was a kaleidoscope of new impressions, of fun, of fear, of freedom and of nagging guilt. Hitting the road, hitchhiking, meeting new people from all over the world.

A flash of memory: French soldiers picking me up at the western outskirts of Stuttgart and hiding me in their garrison near Karlsruhe. They plied me with thick slices of French bread and meaty soups and many questions. They found me "beautiful" and "cultured" and were happy that I could converse with them in a mixture of French, English, and German. They were impressed that I was not afraid and just curious. We sang the simple French songs I had learned in school, and they taught me the Marseillaise. We smoked and discussed our lives. I slept on cots in different dorms and stayed three days before I moved on.

A flash of memory: sitting next to a black GI who was driving a huge truck on the autobahn. He poured his heart out to me about discrimination at home and in the army, about color separation of troops and quarters. I was stunned, having believed until then that racism was strictly an inborn German evil.

A flash of memory: walking along a half-frozen creek, crying with yearning for little Michael, calling his name over and over.

A flash of memory: being dropped off from a jeep at an American installation, with the driver assuring me he would be right back. He wasn't. I stood for an hour or so near the guardhouse, feeling cold, tired, and hungry. Then I fainted. I came to in an ambulance on the way to an infirmary, where I was revived. An American officer took me to his quarters in a large German house for the night. In the morning he sent a German maid who asked me to join him for breakfast in the dining room. I did, but before I could leave he became amorous. I picked up some framed pictures of his wife and children in the States and admired them. His attitude changed soon to glowing descriptions of his family and a growing respect for me. We parted amicably, and he even lent me his car and driver who took me to the next town.

A flash of memory: a cold evening by the autobahn. Still hitchhiking. A United States Army ambulance stopped. It was headed for the spa of Giessen, which lay on my route north to Berlin. It was occupied by five GIs from a medical unit returning from a week's furlough they had spent in Switzerland. It was late when we arrived in Giessen. All were left off, and the driver asked me if I had a place to sleep. When I shook my head he offered me the use of the ambulance for the night and left. In the morning he woke me up with hot chocolate and donuts. We talked while we ate. He was an Episcopal clergyman's son from the city of Binghamton in the state of New York. He had been an engineering student at Purdue University when he was drafted two years ago, and was now 25 years old. He was in charge of all electrical wiring of his unit's mobile field hospital. His name was Ted.

I told him about myself and my intention to somehow get through the border into the Russian sector to Berlin. But when he asked me to stay a day or so I consented.

Alone in his room I washed up and changed my clothes, and he came after work with supper and then we went to the GI club. I disliked alcohol but loved dancing. A live band played those wonderful haunting and—alternating—snappy tunes which I had so loved already when listening to them on my little radio at home. Ted and his friends danced with me slow waltzes, foxtrots and tangos and taught me to jitterbug. Some had brought their German girlfriends. It was warm and exciting and I had my first taste of Coca-Cola. I felt like a happy teenager. When the club closed at 1:00 AM Ted took me to his room, where I spent the night. But he never made a move to touch me. When I left the next morning I promised to try to stop by on my way back...

A flash of memory: Filling out endless forms and waiting in even more endless lines for several days at the
Russian sector border town of Helmstedt. But all my pleading for permission to cross was in vain. An American
driver—who had a border-crossing permit—offered to hide
me in his truck. But I gave up the hope of seeing my parents
in Berlin rather than chancing jail. And, frankly, I was not
especially looking forward to spending time in that huge,
now nearly demolished, and always ugly city of my childhood. Also, by now my worries about baby Michael had
become so all-consuming that I decided to head straight
back to Gmünd.

A flash of memory: An isolated, spooky-looking inn
about halfway on my trip back. A jeep had left me off nearby.
I went inside and used my ration card for a meager meal. A
fat, middle-aged little man was the only other dinner guest.
He came to my table, introduced himself and offered me
some "surplus" ration cards so I could get a piece of cake. I
was still hungry and accepted, but I paid my own bill and
left as soon as possible. I stood by the road to hitchhike
southward when the fat man appeared on a motorcycle and
offered me a ride to the autobahn. It was quite unusual
then for a German to own a motorcycle, much less to have
the gasoline for it. This greasy guy was probably a black-
market specialist. But the urge to move on overcame my
apprehension. I climbed onto the backseat, clutched my
suitcase, and hung on for dear life as he roared off. Just
before we got to the autobahn the fat man veered off onto a
small road, leading into bare, half-frozen fields. I punched
him into the back and yelled for him to stop, which he then
did near a small stand of trees. I was not even surprised
when he demanded payment in the form of sex. I stood
there, towering over him and shaking my head. When he

still moved to open a button on my coat I slapped his face hard. And then I laughed. I laughed 'til the tears rolled down my cheeks, and the more purple he turned with rage the more I laughed. He turned and took off on his smelly machine. I was still grinning as I trudged back about a mile to the autobahn.

A flash of memory: Medieval Nuremberg—not long ago Hitler's favorite city of goose-stepping Nazi parades and of hysterical masses cheering him—where I stopped on my way home. A lawyer friend of mine and his wife had moved there from Gmünd, after the United States Army had taken over their house. I rested for a day at their apartment and they showed me the ancient castle that still stood tall and brooding on a hill in the center of the bombed-out ruins of the city. A castle with numerous medieval torture chambers filled with various unspeakable torture instruments…but what in God's name had we actually learned since then!

Then I was back home. It was still November and I had left only three weeks ago. But little Michael was gone!

After Walter realized I had left he had sent his mother to pick up Michael. So his parents, who had never bothered to see their little grandson, now kept him in their parsonage in the little village not far from the hospital where Walter lived and worked. Odi and Helmut had not dared to stop them.

I called the parents and was told it would be better for the child to live there. Walter had started divorce proceedings, and better food would be available to Michael from their farming parishioners. Also, their loyal maid Maria would help with his care and Walter would be with him whenever he could get away from his duties at the hospital.

I visited Michael at Christmas, but I was watched every minute I spent with him.

Right after Christmas I left Gmünd and headed for Giessen, where Ted was very happy to see me again. I stayed at the local resort hotel, and we dated. After I was there just a few days, Ted's entire medical unit was moved to a town called Eschwege farther north. There we became lovers, and a German family let us live in two rooms of their house, in return for cigarettes, K-rations, and money.

In the spring of 1946 mail and phone service was resumed. What a relief that Father and Mother were still alive! I stayed in constant touch with Odi in Gmünd. She sent me my parent's letters. I did not want to upset them, so I did not give them my change of address.

Ted and I danced almost nightly at the club. During the days I read books by American and British authors. Not only did this improve my English but finally opened my eyes and heart to something other than Nazi-permitted German literature. At times Ted brought me documents from his outfit that needed to be translated from German to English, or vice versa. I took no pay for this since Ted paid the rent and supplemented my food.

When the divorce became final I stayed in Gmünd and traveled to Stuttgart for the proceeding. With my meager resources I paid a lawyer for his advice once, but I faced a hopeless battle for Michael's custody. Walter and his family's well-known and expensive lawyers convinced the judge to declare me the guilty party because I had "left the marriage." For many years I wondered why I had not counter-attacked. But I guess I knew I could not win, because by leaving I had made a major tactical mistake. At least I could visit Michael any time, which I did as often as possible.

Theodore "Ted" John Dewees,
about 1945

After the divorce was final Ted asked me to marry him, and I consented. His unassuming, quiet demeanor, despite his mathematical and technical brilliance, his practical solutions to life's little problems, his generosity, loyalty and masculinity were balm on my frayed nerves, and I felt safe and loved. We knew it would not be easy to become a German "war bride," but we were willing to wait.

There was mixed news from my parents in Berlin. The Russians, who had protected Father in the beginning, were getting tired and angered by Father's mounting criticism of the Communist regime. So he was once again *persona non grata*. One night as he was walking slowly with his cane back home from a visit to a dying parishioner, a gang of thugs attacked and beat him mercilessly. There was no robbery involved, and it was fairly obvious to everyone that these people had been hired. He nearly died of his injuries and spent weeks in the hospital. The Russians refused to investigate the incident and instead ordered Father to stop interfering with their oppressive orders. Mother's health was waning, too. So Father resigned from his East Berlin ministry. He was permitted to move to comfortable quarters in an undestroyed section of West Berlin, and was also given a border-crossing permit so he could visit his former parish anytime.

This does not mean that he quietly slipped into retirement. He asked the Lutheran bishop to let him head the Lutheran ministry in two large German refugee camps on the outskirts of West Berlin. Permission was granted and he was given a car that was altered to accommodate his short leg. He spent the next few years comforting and helping thousands of crammed, depressed, poor, sick and hungry refugee families, opening Kindergartens and hiring visiting nurses. He also fought hard for reuniting families from all over Germany.

It was June 1946. My divorce was final and Ted and I had become engaged. We had just started on our document chase for my exit permit to the United States when his entire medical unit was shipped back to the United States on a large troop ship. He was discharged from the army soon after he returned home.

I moved back into my apartment in Gmünd, for which Helmut was paying the rent now. He had earned his advanced railroad engineering degree and was being rapidly upgraded in positions at the railroad headquarters in Stuttgart. Odi was in her last few months of pregnancy with her second child.

Ted wrote frequently, but my mail to him took forever. He worked hard in the States and I in Germany to arrange permission for me to leave Germany. Many visits by me to the United States consulate in Stuttgart were required.

The hunger and food shortage had gotten even worse now. Ted's widowed mother sent us occasional packages with Crisco, peanut butter, cereal, flour, sugar, and cocoa. Several Mennonite parishes in the United States sent us Care packages, too. We thanked God for the decency of the Americans.

On September 29, Odi's and Helmut's little girl, Christiane, was born. I helped, of course, with the care of mother and babies, while continuing my battle with the slow-moving wheels of American bureaucracy.

We finally got word that Mother's brother, Uncle Engbert, had returned safely to his family in Kassel. And miraculously, Grandmother and her sister Agnes had survived their last-minute flight from the Russian assault on Brieg in Silesia.

The two elderly ladies were now quartered in an old, remodeled castle, along with other refugees, near Würzburg, which is about 100 miles north of Gmünd. More and more trains were finally running again. So I picked up Michael from Walter's parents to introduce him to my grandmother and her sister. My beautiful little boy was now one and a half years old. He was still walking unsteadily and I took his stroller along. I treasured every moment with him, and cried while he slept on my lap.

We arrived at a small railroad station, and I pushed Michael in his stroller down a lane through the forest until we came to a clearing, where the castle was towering.

Grandmother and Aunt Agnes were comfortably quartered in a room all by themselves with a lovely view of parks, fountains and forest. We hugged and kissed and talked and they played with their little great grandson. Nurses brought us some tea and cookies.

It was late when we parted, and the last train had left. Rooms in that village were impossible to get, but an innkeeper let Michael and me sleep on a straw mallet in the maid's quarters. Luckily I had locked the door, because in the middle of the night the drunken innkeeper demanded entry. After he had given up and left, I dressed little Michael and myself silently and quickly, and we sneaked out of the room and the inn. We headed for the railroad station where we spent the rest of the night in the waiting room with other weary travelers. Michael slept soundly in his stroller. The Red Cross served us all some breakfast, and after another tearful train ride I returned Michael safely to Walter's parents, as I had promised.

It was early spring of 1947 now and Ted and I were still struggling with the mysterious ways of bureaucracy. We were beginning to wonder if we would ever be reunited. His congressman in upstate New York finally came to our rescue after Ted appealed to him for help. This politician was able to cut through the Gordian Knot (no entry permit without an exit permit, but no exit permit without an entry permit), and I received my permission to fly to the United States.

Soon thereafter the German Lutheran Church insisted on getting their office back in Gmünd, which I had

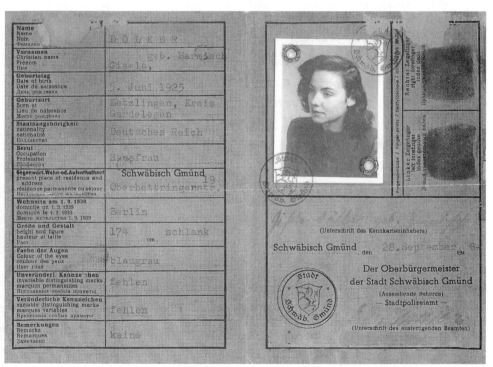

Gisela Dolker Nee Harnisch, age 21. A German "identity card," as required by America.

transformed into my apartment three and a half years ago. Walter's parents had hung on to their half bombed-out apartment in Stuttgart, and they now permitted Odi, Helmut and the two little girls to move in there. I let them have all my furniture, except my grand piano, which I sold to pay for my plane ticket.

In Stuttgart, Helmut helped me to crate my best china, silver, and linen to be shipped to Binghamton, New York, after my arrival there. I stayed with them in Stuttgart 'til my scheduled flight in April.

Father and Mother from Berlin, Uncle Engbert from Kassel, Hugo from Mannheim, and friends from Gmünd and elsewhere came to Stuttgart to bid me farewell. But all my thoughts and tears could not bring Hans and Michael to me...

My entire family accompanied me by train to Frankfurt and to the airport there for tearful good-byes.

It turned out that all my fellow travelers were also war brides, and that we were the first ones to be flown to the United States.

As the TWA plane lifted off, the conflict of searing pain and huge relief tore at me. And so I watched from the window as Germany disappeared and became a memory.

Writings of Interest

For those who wish to extend their reading in connection with the activities of the Confessing Church and resistance to the Third Reich, here are a few suggestions:

Barnett, Victoria. For the Soul of the People: Protestant Protest Against Hitler. New York: Oxford University Press, 1992.

Barnett, Victoria, Director of Church Relations, U.S. Holocaust Memorial Museum, "Dietrich Bonhoeffer," www.ushmm.org/bonhoeffer.

Gilbert, Martin. The Holocaust: The History of the Jews of Europe During the Second World War. New York: Henry Holt and Company, 1985.

Shirer, William. The Rise and Fall of the Third Reich. New York: Simon & Schuster Inc, 1960.

Wind, Renate. Dietrich Bonhoeffer: A Spoke in the Wheel. Grand Rapids, Michigan: Wm. B. Eerdmans Publishing Company, 1992.

Order Form

Please fill out this form (or copy this page), add the necessary information, and mail it to:

DeForest Press
P.O. Box 154
Elk River, MN 55330

Please enclose personal check or money order, payable to: DeForest Press.

Out of Step   by Gisela Dewees $19.95 each
ISBN 1-930374-12-7

Qty. _____   Total: _____

MN residents add 6.5% sales tax ($1.30 / book) _____

Shipping & Handling: Add $2.00 for first book
$1.00 for each additional book   _____

Total enclosed   _____

Name: _____

Address: _____

City: _____ State: _____ Zip: _____

Phone: (_____) _____

Email: _____

_____ Yes, please send me information about your other books, greeting cards, and posters.

You can also order this book and others from our secure web site at: www.DeForestPress.com for immediate delivery.